双语名著无障碍阅读丛书
经典集锦

西方老故事50篇
（旧译 泰西五十轶事）

Fifty Famous Stories Retold

[美] 詹姆斯·鲍德温 编著
郭彧斌 译

中国出版集团
中译出版社

图书在版编目(CIP)数据

西方老故事50篇：英汉对照/(美)詹姆斯·鲍德温（James Baldwin）编著；郭彧斌译. —北京：中译出版社，2018.1（2019.4重印）
（双语名著无障碍阅读丛书）
旧译：泰西五十轶事
ISBN 978-7-5001-5450-1

Ⅰ.①西… Ⅱ.①詹… ②郭… Ⅲ.①英语－汉语－对照读物 ②故事－作品集－世界 Ⅳ.①H319.4：I

中国版本图书馆CIP数据核字(2017)第255206号

出版发行／中译出版社
地　　址／北京市西城区车公庄大街甲4号物华大厦6层
电　　话／(010) 68359827；68359303（发行部）；53601537（编辑部）
邮　　编／100044
传　　真／(010) 68357870
电子邮箱／book@ctph.com.cn
网　　址／http://www.ctph.com.cn

总 策 划／张高里　贾兵伟
策划编辑／胡晓凯
责任编辑／范祥镇　杨　扬

封面设计／潘　峰
排　　版／北京竹页文化传媒有限公司
印　　刷／山东泰安新华印务有限责任公司
经　　销／新华书店

规　　格／710毫米×1000毫米　1/16
印　　张／18.75
字　　数／292千字
版　　次／2018年1月第一版
印　　次／2019年4月第二次

ISBN 978-7-5001-5450-1　定价：29.80元

版权所有　侵权必究
中译出版社

出版前言

多年以来，中译出版社有限公司（原中国对外翻译出版有限公司）凭借国内一流的翻译和出版实力及资源，精心策划、出版了大批双语读物，在海内外读者中和业界内产生了良好、深远的影响，形成了自己鲜明的出版特色。

二十世纪八九十年代出版的英汉（汉英）对照"一百丛书"，声名远扬，成为一套最权威、最有特色且又实用的双语读物，影响了一代又一代英语学习者和中华传统文化研究者、爱好者；还有"英若诚名剧译丛""中华传统文化精粹丛书""美丽英文书系"，这些优秀的双语读物，有的畅销，有的常销不衰反复再版，有的被选为大学英语阅读教材，受到广大读者的喜爱，获得了良好的社会效益和经济效益。

"双语名著无障碍阅读丛书"是中译专门为中学生和英语学习者精心打造的又一品牌，是一个新的双语读物系列，具有以下特点：

选题创新——该系列图书是国内第一套为中小学生量身打造的双语名著读物，所选篇目均为教育部颁布的语文新课标必读书目，或为中学生以及同等文化水平的社会读者喜闻乐见的世界名著，重新编译为英汉（汉英）对照的双语读本。这些书既给青少年读者提供了成长过程中不可或缺的精神食粮，又让他们领略到原著的精髓和魅力，对他们更好地学习英文大有裨益；同时，丛书中入选的《论语》《茶馆》《家》等汉英对照读物，亦是热爱中国传统文化的中外读者所共知的经典名篇，能使读者充分享受阅读经典的无限乐趣。

无障碍阅读——中学生阅读世界文学名著的原著会遇到很多生词和文化难点。针对这一情况，我们给每一本读物原文中的较难词汇和不易理解之处都加上了注释，在内文的版式设计上也采取英汉（或汉英）对照方式，扫清了学生阅读时的障碍。

优良品质——中译双语读物多年来在读者中享有良好口碑，这得益于作者和出版者对于图书质量的不懈追求。"双语名著无障碍阅读丛书"继承了中译双语读物的优良传统——精选的篇目、优秀的译文、方便实用的注解，秉承着对每一个读者负责的精神，竭力打造精品图书。

愿这套丛书成为广大读者的良师益友，愿读者在英语学习和传统文化学习两方面都取得新的突破。

目录 CONTENTS

1. King Alfred and the Cakes

1. 阿尔弗雷德国王和蛋糕 ················ 003

2. King Alfred and the Beggar

2. 阿尔弗雷德国王和乞丐 ················ 009

3. King Canute on the Seashore

3. 克努特国王在海滨 ···················· 013

4. The Sons of William the Conqueror

4. 征服者威廉的儿子们 ·················· 019

5. The White Ship

5. 白色的帆船 ·························· 025

6. King John and the Abbot

6. 约翰国王和修道院院长 ················ 033

7. A Story of Robin Hood

7. 罗宾汉的故事 ························ 043

目录 CONTENTS

8. Bruce and the Spider
8. 布鲁斯国王和蜘蛛 ………………………………… 051

9. The Black Douglas
9. 黑面人道格拉斯 …………………………………… 055

10. Three Men of Gotham
10. 三个哥坦人 ………………………………………… 061

11. Other Wise Men of Gotham
11. 哥坦城其他的聪明人 ……………………………… 067

12. The Miller of the Dee
12. 迪水河畔的磨坊主 ………………………………… 075

13. Sir Philip Sidney
13. 菲利普·锡德尼爵士 ……………………………… 079

14. The Ungrateful Soldier
14. 忘恩负义的士兵 …………………………………… 083

15. Sir Humphrey Gilbert
15. 汉弗莱·吉尔伯特爵士 …………………………… 087

16. Sir Walter Raleigh
16. 沃尔特·雷利爵士 ………………………………… 089

目录 CONTENTS

17. Pocahontas
17. 波卡洪塔斯 ……………………………… 095

18. George Washington and His Hatchet
18. 乔治•华盛顿和他的小斧头 ……………… 099

19. Grace Darling
19. 格蕾丝•达琳 …………………………… 103

20. The Story of William Tell
20. 威廉•泰尔的故事 ……………………… 107

21. Arnold Winkelried
21. 阿诺德•温克里德 ……………………… 111

22. The Bell of Atri
22. 阿特里的钟 ……………………………… 115

23. How Napoleon Crossed the Alps
23. 拿破仑翻越阿尔卑斯山 ………………… 125

24. The Story of Cincinnatus
24. 辛辛那图斯的故事 ……………………… 129

25. The Story of Regulus
25. 雷古鲁斯的故事 ………………………… 137

目录 CONTENTS

26. Cornelia's Jewels
26. 科妮莉娅的珠宝 ………………………… 143

27. Androclus and the Lion
27. 安德洛克鲁斯和狮子 …………………… 147

28. Horatius at the Bridge
28. 桥上的贺雷修斯 ………………………… 153

29. Julius Cæsar
29. 尤利乌斯·恺撒 ………………………… 159

30. The Sword of Damocles
30. 达摩克利斯之剑 ………………………… 163

31. Damon and Pythias
31. 达蒙和皮西厄斯 ………………………… 169

32. A Laconic Answer
32. 简洁的回答 ……………………………… 173

33. The Ungrateful Guest
33. 忘恩负义的客人 ………………………… 177

34. Alexander and Bucephalus
34. 亚历山大和布西发拉斯 ………………… 181

目录 CONTENTS

35. Diogenes the Wise Man
35. 智者第欧根尼 ………………………………… 185

36. The Brave Three Hundred
36. 三百名勇士 …………………………………… 189

37. Socrates and His House
37. 苏格拉底和他的房子 ………………………… 193

38. The King and His Hawk
38. 国王和鹰 ……………………………………… 195

39. Doctor Goldsmith
39. 戈德史密斯医生 ……………………………… 203

40. The Kingdoms
40. 王国 …………………………………………… 207

41. The Barmecide Feast
41. 巴米赛德的盛宴 ……………………………… 213

42. The Endless Tale
42. 讲不完的故事 ………………………………… 219

43. The Blind Men and the Elephant
43. 盲人摸象 ……………………………………… 225

目录 CONTENTS

44. Maximilian and the Goose Boy
44. 麦克西米利安和放鹅的小孩 ·················· 229

45. The Inchcape Rock
45. 印奇开普暗礁 ······························ 237

46. Whittington and His Cat
46. 威廷顿和他的猫 ···························· 243

47. Casabianca
47. 卡萨比安卡 ································ 261

48. Antonio Canova
48. 安东尼奥·卡诺瓦 ·························· 267

49. Picciola
49. 皮丘拉 ···································· 275

50. Mignon
50. 美格珑 ···································· 283

James Baldwin

1. King Alfred and the Cakes

Many years ago there lived in England a wise and good king whose name was Alfred. No other man ever did so much for his country as he; and people now, all over the world, speak of him as Alfred the Great.

In those days a king did not have a very easy life. There was war almost all the time, and no one else could lead his army into battle so well as he. And so, between ruling and fighting, he had a busy time of it indeed.

A **fierce**[①], **rude**[②] people, called the Danes, had come from over the sea, and

1. 阿尔弗雷德国王和蛋糕

许多年前，英格兰有一位睿智善良的国王名叫阿尔弗雷德。这个国王为国家作出的贡献无人能比，世人现在谈起他，都将他称为阿尔弗雷德大帝。

在当时那个年代，做国王的日子并不好过。由于战争连绵不断，阿尔弗雷德领兵打仗的本领又无人能敌，所以他一方面要治理国家，另一方面还要带兵打仗，阿尔弗雷德国王实在太忙了。

有一个名叫"丹麦"的残暴野蛮的民族，远渡重洋

① fierce [fiəs] *a.* 凶猛的
② rude [ru:d] *a.* 野蛮的

were fighting the English. There were so many of them, and they were so bold and strong, that for a long time they gained every battle. If they kept on, they would soon be the masters of the whole country.

At last, after a great battle, the English army was broken up and **scattered**①. Every man had to save himself in the best way he could. King Alfred **fled**② alone, in great **haste**③, through the woods and swamps.

Late in the day the king came to the **hut**④ of a **woodcutter**⑤. He was very tired and hungry, and he begged the woodcutter's wife to give him something to eat and a place to sleep in her hut.

The woman was baking some cakes upon the **hearth**⑥, and she looked with pity upon the poor, ragged fellow who seemed so hungry. She had no thought that he was the king.

"Yes," she said, "I will give you some supper if you will watch these cakes. I want to go out and milk the cow; and you must see that they do not burn while I am gone."

King Alfred was very willing to watch the cakes, but he had far greater things to think about. How was he going to get his army together again? And how was he going to drive the fierce Danes out of the land? He forgot his hunger; he forgot the cakes; he forgot that he was in the woodcutter's hut. His mind was busy making plans for tomorrow.

In a little while the woman came back. The cakes were smoking on the hearth. They were burned to a **crisp**⑦. Ah, how angry she was!

"You lazy fellow!" she cried. "See what you have done! You want something to eat, but you do not want to work!"

I have been told that she even struck the king with a stick; but I can hardly believe that she was so **ill-natured**⑧.

The king must have laughed to himself at the thought of being scolded in this way; and he was so hungry that he did not mind the woman's angry words half so much as the loss of the cakes.

① scattered ['skætəd] *a.* 溃散的
② fled [fled] *v.*（flee 的过去式）逃跑
③ haste [heist] *n.* 仓促
④ hut [hʌt] *n.* 小屋
⑤ woodcutter ['wud,kʌtə(r)] *n.* 伐木者
⑥ hearth [hɑ:θ] *n.* 壁炉

⑦ crisp [krisp] *n.* 松脆物

⑧ ill-natured ['il-neitʃəd] *a.* 脾气坏的

攻打英国。他们人多势众，胆大凶猛，在很长一段时间里他们逢战必胜。如果照此形势发展下去，整个英国恐怕不久就要落入他们的手中。

在后来的一场恶战中，英国军队被打散了，士兵们纷纷逃走以寻求自保。阿尔弗雷德国王逃走的时候只有孤身一人，他行色匆匆地从树林和沼泽中间穿行而过。

夜幕降临。国王来到一个伐木工住的小木屋，当时他又累又饿，请求伐木工的妻子给他弄点吃的，并且允许他在那里过夜。

女主人正忙着在火炉上烤蛋糕，她同情地看着眼前这个衣衫褴褛、饥肠辘辘的可怜家伙，丝毫没有想到此人竟会是国王陛下。

"好吧！"她说，"只要你帮我看着这些蛋糕，我就给你晚饭吃。我现在出去挤牛奶，我不在的时候你要看着蛋糕，别把它们烤煳了。"

阿尔弗雷德国王当然很乐意帮这个忙，可是他还有更重要的事情需要考虑，比如怎样才能把溃散的军队集合起来，怎样把凶恶的丹麦人赶出国土。想着想着，他竟然忘记了饥饿，忘记了蛋糕，忘记了自己身处伐木工的小木屋里，满脑子都是第二天的行动计划。

过了一会儿，女主人回来了。看见蛋糕已经烤成焦炭在炉子上冒着烟，她当时就火冒三丈！

"你这个懒鬼！"她大声训斥道，"看你干的好事！你想吃东西，可什么都不想干！"

我听人说她最后居然还抄起棍子打了国王。不过，我真的无法相信她的性情竟然会如此暴躁。

国王想到自己竟然受到这样的责骂，心里一定会暗自发笑。当时他实在太饿了，因此比起女主人的责骂，他更懊恼的是烤煳了的蛋糕。

· 005 ·

I do not know whether he had anything to eat that night, or whether he had to go to bed without his supper. But it was not many days until he had gathered his men together again, and had beaten the Danes in a great battle.

那天晚上国王到底有没有吃到东西我并不清楚,也许他饿着肚子就睡了。但是此后不久,他集合起自己的军队,在一场大战中打败了丹麦人。

2. King Alfred and the Beggar

At one time the Danes drove King Alfred from his kingdom, and he had to lie hidden for a long time on a little island in a river.

One day, all who were on the island, except the king and queen and one servant, went out to fish. It was a very lonely place, and no one could get to it except by a boat. About noon a ragged beggar came to the king's door, and asked for food.

The king called the servant, and asked, "How much food have we in the house?"

"My lord," said the servant, "we have only one **loaf**[1] and a little wine."

Then the king gave thanks to God, and said, "Give half of the loaf and half of the wine to this poor man."

The servant did as he was **bidden**[2]. The beggar thanked the king for his kindness, and went on his way.

In the afternoon the men who had gone out to fish came back. They had three boats full of fish, and they said, "We have caught more fish today than in all the other days that we have been on this island."

The king was glad, and he and his people were more hopeful than they had ever been before.

When night came, the king lay awake for a long time, and thought about the

2. 阿尔弗雷德国王和乞丐

丹麦人曾经一度将阿尔弗雷德国王赶出了他自己的国家，他被迫在一个河心岛上隐匿了很长时间。

一天，岛上除了留下国王、王后和一个仆人外，所有人都出去打鱼了。这个小岛的位置十分偏僻，只有乘船才能到达。大约中午时分，一个衣衫褴褛的乞丐来到国王门前讨饭。

国王叫来仆人，问道："家里还有多少吃的？"

"主人，"仆人回答说，"只剩下一条面包和一点酒了。"

国王感谢完上帝后说："把面包和酒分一半给这个可怜的人吧！"

仆人照着他的吩咐做了。乞丐谢过国王后，又继续上路了。

下午，出去打鱼的人满载而归，并且运回来整整三条船的鱼。他们说："自从我们来到这个岛上，今天抓到的鱼是最多的一次。"

国王十分高兴，他和随从们对未来都充满了前所未有的信心。

夜幕降临时分，国王想着那天发生的事情，许久不

① loaf [ləuf] n. 长面包

② bidden ['bidən] v.（bid 的过去分词）要求

things that had happened that day. At last he **fancied**① that he saw a great light like the sun; and in the midst of the light there stood an old man with black hair, holding an open book in his hand.

It may all have been a dream, and yet to the king it seemed very real indeed. He looked and wondered, but was not afraid.

"Who are you?" he asked of the old man.

"Alfred, my son, be brave," said the man; "for I am the one to whom you gave this day the half of all the food that you had. Be strong and joyful of heart, and listen to what I say. Rise up early in the morning and blow your **horn**② three times, so loudly that the Danes may hear it. By nine o'clock, five hundred men will be around you ready to be led into battle. Go forth bravely, and within seven days your enemies shall be beaten, and you shall go back to your kingdom to **reign**③ in peace."

Then the light went out, and the man was seen no more.

In the morning the king arose early, and crossed over to the mainland. Then he blew his horn three times very loudly; and when his friends heard it they were glad, but the Danes were filled with fear.

At nine o'clock, five hundred of his bravest soldiers stood around him ready for battle. He spoke, and told them what he had seen and heard in his dream; and when he had finished, they all cheered loudly, and said that they would follow him and fight for him so long as they had strength.

So they went out bravely to battle; and they beat the Danes, and drove them back into their own place. And King Alfred ruled wisely and well over all his people for the rest of his days.

① fancy ['fænsi] v. 想象

② horn [hɔːn] n. 号角

③ reign [rein] v. 统治

能入睡。恍恍惚惚中，他看到一束光，像太阳一样明亮，里面站着一位黑发老人，手里拿着一本打开的书。

这可能完完全全就是个梦，可是对于国王而言，它却非常真实。他望着那个老人，心里有些疑惑，可并没有感到恐惧。

"你是谁？"他向那个老人问道。

"阿尔弗雷德，我的孩子，不要害怕，"老人说，"我就是今天你分给一半食物的那个人。你要坚强起来，乐观起来。听我说，明天早晨要早早起来吹响三声号角，要使劲地吹，要让丹麦人听见。九点钟的时候会有500个人来到你的身边，准备跟随你冲锋陷阵。要勇敢地向前冲，七天之内敌人就会被打败，你将重回王位，在和平中统治自己的国家。"

说完这些，那道亮光消失了，老人也不见了。

第二天，国王一大早就起身，乘船回到陆地上，他用力吹响了三声号角。朋友们听到他的号角声都感到非常振奋，而丹麦人听见了却吓破了胆。

九点时分，国王和五百名最勇敢的士兵站在一起准备迎接战斗。他把自己在睡梦中的所见所闻讲给士兵们听；他们听完故事后大声欢呼，说哪怕还有一丝气力，就要跟随他一起战斗。

就这样，国王率领他的士兵英勇地奔赴战场，他们打败了丹麦人，并且把丹麦人赶回了老家。从此以后，在他的有生之年里，阿尔弗雷德国王英明地统治着自己的国家。

3. King Canute on the Seashore

A hundred years or more after the time of Alfred the Great there was a king of England named Canute. King Canute was a Dane; but the Danes were not so fierce and cruel then as they had been when they were at war with King Alfred.

The great men and officers who were around King Canute were always praising him.

"You are the greatest man that ever lived," one would say.

Then another would say, "O king! There can never be another man so **mighty**① as you."

And another would say, "Great Canute, there is nothing in the world that dares to disobey you."

The king was a man of sense, and he grew very tired of hearing such foolish speeches.

One day he was by the seashore, and his officers were with him. They were praising him, as they were in the habit of doing. He thought that now he would teach them a lesson, and so he bade them set his chair on the beach close by the edge of the water.

"Am I the greatest man in the world?" he asked.

"O king!" they cried, "there is no one so mighty as you."

"Do all things obey me?" he asked.

3. 克努特国王在海滨

阿尔弗雷德大帝的时代过去一百多年后，英格兰有一个国王名叫克努特。克努特国王是丹麦人，可是当时的丹麦人已经变得不像和阿尔弗雷德国王交战时那样凶猛残暴。

克努特国王身边的达官显贵们总在极力奉承他。

"从古至今您是最伟大的人。"一个人如此说道。

接着另一个人又说："啊，国王陛下！今后不会再有人像您一样强大了。"

还有人会说："伟大的克努特国王，世上没有什么东西敢违抗您的旨意。"

国王是一个理智的人。对于这些愚蠢的吹捧，他越来越感到厌倦。

一天，官员们跟随国王一起来到海滨，他们又像往常那样开始恭维他。克努特想，现在是时候给他们点教训了。于是，他让人把椅子放在海滩上靠近大海的地方。

"我是世界上最伟大的人吗？"他问。

"噢，国王陛下！"他们高声说，"没有人比您更伟大了。"

"万物都会臣服于我吗？"他又问。

① mighty ['maiti] *a.* 强大的

"There is nothing that dares to disobey you, O king!" they said.

"The world bows before you, and gives you honor."

"Will the sea obey me?" he asked; and he looked down at the little waves which were lapping the sand at his feet.

The foolish officers were puzzled, but they did not dare to say "No."

"Command it, O king! and it will obey," said one.

"Sea," cried Canute, "I command you to come no farther! Waves, stop your rolling, and do not dare to touch my feet!"

"Sea, I command you to come no farther!"

But the tide came in, just as it always did. The water rose higher and higher. It came up around the king's chair, and wet not only his feet, but also his **robe**①. His officers stood about him, alarmed, and wondering whether he was not mad.

"噢,国王陛下!没有什么东西胆敢违抗您。"他们回答说。

"整个世界都在要您面前弯腰,向您致敬。"

"大海也会听从我的调遣吗?"他又问,同时低头看着脚下拍打着沙子的小浪花。

那些愚蠢的官员们面面相觑,可是谁都不敢说一个"不"字。

"啊,国王陛下,只要您下命令,大海一定会听您调遣的。"一个人说。

"大海,"克努特大声喊道,"我要你停止前进!波浪,我要你停下来,不要再冲刷我的脚!"

"大海,我要你停止前进!"

① robe [rəub] *n.* 长袍

可是波浪依然像往常一样继续向上涨。海水越涨越高,一直漫到国王的座椅旁边,把他的脚打湿了,还弄湿了他的长袍。官员们站在旁边吓得目瞪口呆,担心国王发疯了。

· 015 ·

Then Canute took off his crown, and threw it down upon the sand.

"I shall never wear it again," he said. "And do you, my men, learn a lesson from what you have seen. There is only one King who is all-powerful; and it is he who rules the sea, and holds the ocean in the hollow of his hand. It is he whom you ought to praise and serve above all others."

克努特摘掉王冠扔在沙滩上。

"从今以后我再也不戴这顶王冠了。"他说,"我的臣子们,你们要从刚才的那一幕吸取教训!世界上只有一个万能的王,他主宰着大海,将海洋握在手心,他才是你们应该赞扬和服侍的人。"

4. The Sons of William the Conqueror

There was once a great king of England who was called William the Conqueror, and he had three sons.

One day King William seemed to be thinking of something that made him feel very sad; and the wise men who were about him asked him what was the matter.

"I am thinking," he said, "of what my sons may do after I am dead. For, unless they are wise and strong, they cannot keep the kingdom which I have won for them. Indeed, I am at a loss to know which one of the three ought to be the king when I am gone."

"O king!" said the wise men, "if we only knew what things your sons admire the most, we might then be able to tell what kind of men they will be. Perhaps, by asking each one of them a few questions, we can find out which one of them will be best fitted to rule in your place."

"The plan is well worth trying, at least," said the king. "Have the boys come before you, and then ask them what you please."

The wise men talked with one another for a little while, and then agreed that the young princes should be brought in, one at a time, and that the same questions should be put to each.

The first who came into the room was Robert. He was a tall, willful **lad**①, and was nick-named Short Stocking.

4. 征服者威廉的儿子们

从前,英格兰有一个伟大的国王,人们称他为征服者威廉。威廉国王有三个儿子。

一天,威廉国王似乎想到了什么,心里感到十分难过。身边的一些智者便问他到底为什么事而感到伤心。

"我在想,"国王说,"我死了以后,我的儿子们该怎么办。如果他们没有智慧,没有力量,就守不住我为他们打下的江山。而且我死后,也不知道他们三个谁能做国王。"

"啊,国王陛下!"智者们说,"如果能够知道他们每个人心目中最崇拜什么,兴许就能知道他们的将来。也许问他们每个人一些问题,就能够知道谁将来最适合做国王。"

"这个想法倒是值得试一试!"国王说,"去把孩子们叫来,你们想问什么就问什么。"

智者们商议了片刻,决定每次只让一个王子进来,要问的问题也都一模一样。

罗伯特王子第一个进来,他个子高,个性张扬,绰号"短袜"。

---

① lad [læd] n. 少年,小伙子

"Fair sir," said one of the men, "answer me this question: If, instead of being a boy, it had pleased God that you should be a bird, what kind of a bird would you rather be?"

"A **hawk**①," answered Robert. "I would rather be a hawk, for no other bird reminds one so much of a bold and **gallant**② knight."

The next who came was young William, his father's name-sake and pet. His face was **jolly**③ and round, and because he had red hair he was nicknamed **Rufus**④, or the Red.

"Fair sir," said the wise man, "answer me this question: If, instead of being a boy, it had pleased God that you should be a bird, what kind of a bird would you rather be?"

"An **eagle**⑤," answered William. "I would rather be an eagle, because it is strong and brave. It is feared by all other birds, and is therefore the king of them all."

Lastly came the youngest brother, Henry, with quiet steps and a sober, thoughtful look. He had been taught to read and write, and for that reason he was nicknamed Beau Clerc, or the Handsome Scholar.

"Fair sir," said the wise man, "answer me this question: If, instead of being a boy, it had pleased God that you should be a bird, what kind of a bird would you rather be?"

"A **starling**⑥," said Henry. "I would rather be a starling, because it is good-mannered and kind and a joy to every one who sees it, and it never tries to rob or abuse its neighbor."

Then the wise men talked with one another for a little while, and when they had agreed among themselves, they spoke to the king.

"We find," said they, "that your eldest son, Robert, will be bold and gallant. He will do some great deeds, and make a name for himself; but in the end he will be overcome by his **foes**⑦, and will die in prison.

"The second son, William, will be as brave and strong as the eagle; but he will be feared and hated for his cruel deeds. He will lead a **wicked**⑧ life, and will

① hawk [hɔ:k] *n.* 鹰
② gallant ['gælənt] *a.* 英勇的

③ jolly ['dʒɔli] *a.* 愉快的
④ Rufus ['ru:fəs] *n.* 〔口语〕"红毛"（对红头发人的称呼）

⑤ eagle ['i:gl] *n.* 雕

⑥ starling ['stɑ:liŋ] *n.* 燕八哥

⑦ foe ['fəu] *n.* 敌人
⑧ wicked ['wikid] *a.* 邪恶的

"王子殿下，"一个智者问道，"请问：如果上帝想让您变成一只鸟而不是人，您最想成为哪种鸟？"

"我想成为老鹰，"罗伯特王子回答道，"在所有的鸟里面，只有老鹰才能和英勇无畏的骑士相比。"

威廉王子第二个进来。他和父王同名，深得父王的宠爱。威廉王子性情乐观愉悦，圆脸，满头红发，因此绰号"红头发"。

"王子殿下，"智者又问，"请问：如果上帝想让您变成一只鸟而不是人，您最想成为哪种鸟？"

"我想做大雕，"威廉王子回答道，"大雕威武凶猛，别的鸟儿都害怕它，大雕才是百鸟之王。"

最后进来的是亨利王子。他年纪最轻，却步履沉稳，神情稳重，脸上带着一副若有所思的表情。亨利王子受过教育，能读会写，因此绰号"英俊的学者"。

"王子殿下，"智者继续问道，"请问：如果上帝想让您变成一只鸟而不是人，您最想成为哪种鸟？"

"我想成为一只八哥，"亨利王子回答说。"八哥对人友善，举止文雅，它总能给见到它的人带来欢乐，而且绝不害人。"

随后智者们又围在一起商议了片刻，达成一致的看法后，他们对国王说：

"我们认为您的大儿子罗伯特长大后将是一个胆大无畏的人，他会有一番作为，也能为自己扬名立威，可是最终恐怕要被敌人打败，死于牢狱之中。

"您的二儿子威廉会像大雕一样威猛勇敢，但是他凶残邪恶，恐将招人痛恨，死的时候会遭到万人的唾骂。"

die a shameful death.

"The youngest son, Henry, will be wise and **prudent**① and peaceful. He will go to war only when he is forced to do so by his enemies. He will be loved at home, and respected abroad; and he will die in peace after having gained great possessions."

Years passed by, and the three boys had grown up to be men. King William lay upon his **deathbed**②, and again he thought of what would become of his sons when he was gone. Then he remembered what the wise men had told him; and so he declared that Robert should have the lands which he held in France, that William should be the King of England, and that Henry should have no land at all, but only a **chest**③ of gold.

So it happened in the end very much as the wise men had foretold. Robert, the Short Stocking, was bold and reckless, like the hawk which he so much admired. He lost all the lands that his father had left him, and was at last shut up in prison, where he was kept until he died.

William Rufus was so overbearing and cruel that he was feared and hated by all his people. He led a wicked life, and was killed by one of his own men while hunting in the forest.

And Henry, the Handsome Scholar, had not only the chest of gold for his own, but he became by and by the King of England and the ruler of all the lands that his father had had in France.

① prudent ['pru:dənt] *a.* 谨慎的

② deathbed ['deθbed] *n.* 临终（时睡的）床

③ chest [tʃest] *n.* 箱子

"您的小儿子亨利聪明沉稳，生性平和，不到迫不得已是不会轻易挑起战争的。亨利王子将受到人民的喜爱、外邦的敬仰，功名卓著，最后安然离世。"

几年过去了，三个王子均长大成人。在弥留之际，威廉国王又想起自己死后儿子们该怎么办，智者们说的那些话他没有忘记。因此他宣布把自己在法国的领地赐给罗伯特，让威廉做英格兰的国王，而给亨利却没有分一寸土地，只给了他一箱黄金。

故事最后的结局果然不出智者们的预料。长大后，"短袜"罗伯特性格胆大狂妄，就像他崇拜的老鹰那样，最后不仅葬送了父王留给他的所有土地，而且还被关进大牢，死于牢狱之中。

"红头发"威廉傲慢残暴，生性邪恶，人民对他又惧又恨；有一次他去森林里打猎，遭到了手下人的暗算。

而"英俊的学者"亨利则不但守住了自己的黄金，后来还当了英格兰的国王，父王在法国的所有土地最后也为他所有。

5. The White Ship

King Henry, the Handsome Scholar, had one son, named William, whom he dearly loved. The young man was noble and brave, and everybody hoped that he would some day be the King of England.

One summer Prince William went with his father across the sea to look after their lands in France. They were welcomed with joy by all their people there, and the young prince was so gallant and kind, that he won the love of all who saw him.

But at last the time came for them to go back to England. The king, with his wise men and brave knights, set sail early in the day; but Prince William with his younger friends waited a little while. They had had so joyous a time in France that they were in no great haste to tear themselves away.

Then they went on board of the ship which was waiting to carry them home. It was a beautiful ship with white sails and white **masts**[①], and it had been fitted up on purpose for this voyage.

The sea was smooth, the winds were fair, and no one thought of danger. On the ship, everything had been arranged to make the trip a pleasant one. There was music and dancing, and everybody was merry and glad.

The sun had gone down before the white-winged vessel was fairly out of the bay. But what of that? The moon was at its full, and it would give light enough;

5. 白色的帆船

威廉是"英俊的学者"亨利国王的儿子，深得国王的宠爱。这个年轻人品行高尚，勇敢无畏，人们都盼望着有朝一日，他能够成为英格兰的国王。

有一年夏天，威廉王子跟随父亲乘船前往法国照看那里的领地，国王父子的到来受到了当地人的热烈欢迎。年轻的王子既英勇又仁慈，凡是见到他的人都对他充满了敬意。

可是回家的日子最后还是到了。当天，国王带着智者和武士乘船先行启程，留下威廉王子和一些年轻人稍晚一些时间离开。这次法国之行非常愉快，真的到要离开的时候大家都依依不舍。

最后，大家还是登上了回家的那艘帆船，这艘漂亮的帆船上树立着白色的船帆和桅杆，是专门为这次法国之行建造的。

当时海面上风平浪静，让人丝毫感觉不到会出现什么异样。船上的一切也都安排得妥妥当当，以确保这次旅行平安愉快。伴随着音乐声，人们载歌载舞，尽情欢笑。

夕阳西下。白色的帆船徐徐驶出海湾，一轮圆月将银色的月光洒向海面。如果不出意外，次日黎明，船就

① mast [mɑːst; mæst] n. 船桅

Fifty Famous Stories Retold

and before the dawn of the morrow, the narrow sea would be crossed. And so the prince, and the young people who were with him, gave themselves up to **merriment**① and **feasting**② and joy.

The earlier hours of the night passed by; and then there was a cry of alarm on **deck**③. A moment after-ward there was a great crash. The ship had struck upon a rock. The water rushed in. She was sinking. Ah, where now were those who had lately been so heart-free and glad?

Every heart was full of fear. No one knew what to do. A small boat was quickly launched, and the prince with a few of his bravest friends leaped into it. They pushed off just as the ship was beginning to settle beneath the waves. Would they be saved?

They had rowed hardly ten yards from the ship, when there was a cry from among those that were left behind.

"Row back!" cried the prince. "It is my little sister. She must be saved!"

The men did not dare to disobey. The boat was again brought alongside of the sinking vessel. The prince stood up, and held out his arms for his sister. At that moment the ship gave a great lurch forward into the waves. One **shriek**④ of terror was heard, and then all was still **save**⑤ the sound of the **moaning**⑥ waters.

Ship and boat, prince and princess, and all the gay company that had set sail from France, went down to the bottom together. One man clung to a floating **plank**⑦, and was saved the next day. He was the only person left alive to tell the sad story.

When King Henry heard of the death of his son his grief was more than he could bear. His heart was broken. He had no more joy in life; and men say that no one ever saw him smile again.

Here is a poem about him that your teacher may read to you, and perhaps, after a while, you may learn it by heart.

① merriment ['merimənt] n. 欢乐
② feasting [fi:stiŋ] v. (feast 的现在分词形式) 享用盛宴
③ deck [dek] n. 甲板

④ shriek [ʃri:k] n. 尖叫
⑤ save [seiv] prep. 除了……以外
⑥ moaning [məuniŋ] v. (moaning 是 moan 的现在分词形式) 呻吟
⑦ plank [plæŋk] n. 厚板

能跨过这片狭窄的海域。想到这些，王子和随行的人员心情便十分愉快，禁不住开怀畅饮起来。

夜色渐浓，甲板上突然传来了警报声；片刻之间，伴随着一声巨响，船便撞上了礁石，海水开始涌入，船也开始慢慢下沉。啊呀，几分钟前还无忧无虑、心情欢畅的人们现在在哪里啊？

此刻所有人都被吓破了胆，谁也不知道该怎么办。很快，一艘小船被放到海面上，王子带着一些最勇敢的朋友跳到小船上，他们一直等到大船即将要被海浪吞没才离开。他们能得救吗？

小船刚刚往前划行不到几十米远，大船上突然传来一阵哭声。

"快划回去！"王子叫道。"那是我妹妹，一定要去救她！"

没有人敢违抗王子的命令。小船随即返回到即将沉没的大船旁边，王子站起身张开双臂想抱住妹妹，可是突然之间，大船的船身猛然向前摇晃了一下便沉入海中。一阵恐惧的尖叫声之后，海面上除了海水的悲鸣声，一切复归平静。

大船和小船，王子和公主，还有那些一同离开法国的快乐伙伴们全都沉入了海底。只有一个人第二天得救，当时他抓住了漂在海面上的一块木板，成为全船唯一的幸存者，讲述了这个悲伤的故事。

王子的噩耗传来，亨利国王悲痛欲绝，生命中从此没有了欢乐。人们说从那以后，就再也没有见过他露出笑容。

下面这首诗描写的就是亨利国王，老师也许会读给你们听。也许要不了多久，你们就能把它背下来。

HE NEVER SMILED AGAIN.

The **bark**① that held the prince went down,
  The sweeping waves rolled on;
And what was England's glorious crown
  To him that **wept**② a son?
He lived, for life may long be borne
  Ere sorrow breaks its chain:
Why comes not death to those who mourn?
  He never smiled again.

There stood proud forms before his throne,
  The **stately**③ and the brave;
But who could fill the place of one,—
  That one beneath the wave?
Before him passed the young and fair,
  In pleasure's reckless train;
But seas dashed **o'er**④ his son's bright hair—
  He never smiled again.

He sat where **festal**⑤ bowls went round;
  He heard the **minstrel**⑥ sing;
He saw the tourney's victor crowned
  Amid the knightly ring.
A murmur of the restless deep
  Was blent with every strain,
A voice of winds that would not sleep—
  He never smiled again.

Hearts, in that time, closed o'er the trace

从此不见了他的笑颜

王子的小船沉没海上,
汹涌的波浪还在鸣唱;
英格兰的王冠荣耀无上
又怎能抵上国王痛失爱子之殇?
活着就要长久忍耐
悲伤冲破锁链又添新的无奈;
死神为何不降临到这些哀伤者的身上?——
从此不见了他的笑颜!

王位旁的大臣形象
骄傲庄严又有胆量;
可又有谁能比得上,
沉睡在波浪下王子的模样?
年轻才俊从他的身旁走过,
快乐而无拘无束的模样;
可海水没过了儿子闪亮的头发之上——
从此不见了他的笑颜!

他坐在摆着节日酒杯旋转着的桌旁,
他听着游吟歌手的欢唱;
他看见锦标赛胜利者的冠带
在环形的骑士竞技场上:
大海深处烦躁不安的喧响
与种种伤痛纠缠抵抗,
风的声音不会停止鸣唱:
从此不见了他的笑颜!

心门紧闭不忍再勾起悲伤

① bark [bɑːk] *n.* [古语、诗歌用语] 船
② wept [wept] *v.* (weep 的过去式) 哭泣
③ stately ['steitli] *a.* 庄严的
④ o'er ['əuvə] over 的缩略形式
⑤ festal ['festl] *a.* 节日的
⑥ minstrel ['minstrəl] *n.* 吟游诗人

> Of vows once fondly poured,
> And strangers took the kinsman's place
> At many a joyous board;
> Graves which true love had bathed with tears
> Were left to heaven's bright rain;
> Fresh hopes were born for other years —
> He never smiled again!
>
> MRS. HEMANS.

胸中曾经流淌着怜爱的句章；
陌生人占据了亲人的地方
在许多欢乐的甲板之上；
曾经被至爱泪水浸透的坟场，
闪烁着天堂之雨的明亮；
新的希望将在来年绽放——
从此不见了他的笑颜！

——希曼夫人

6. King John and the Abbot

I. THE THREE QUESTIONS.

There was once a king of England whose name was John. He was a bad king; for he was harsh and cruel to his people, and so long as he could have his own way, he did not care what became of other folks. He was the worst king that England ever had.

Now, there was in the town of Canterbury a rich old **abbot**① who lived in grand style in a great house called the Abbey. Every day a hundred noble men sat down with him to dine; and fifty brave knights, in fine velvet coats and gold chains, waited upon him at his table.

When King John heard of the way in which the abbot lived, he made up his mind to put a stop to it. So he sent for the old man to come and see him.

"How now, my good abbot?" he said. "I hear that you keep a far better house than I. How dare you do such a thing? Don't you know that no man in the land ought to live better than the king? And I tell you that no man shall."

"O king!" said the abbot, "I beg to say that I am spending nothing but what is my own. I hope that you will not think ill of me for making things pleasant for my friends and the brave knights who are with me."

"Think ill of you?" said the king. "How can I help but think ill of you? All that there is in this broad land is mine by right; and how do you dare to put me to

6. 约翰国王和修道院院长

（1）国王的三个问题

从前，英格兰有一位约翰国王。他对待人民冷酷残暴、为所欲为，并且丝毫不把百姓的疾苦放在心上，堪称英格兰历史上最坏的国王。

当时，坎特伯雷城住着一位修道院老院长。此人非常富有，住在富丽堂皇的修道院里面，每天要和一百名贵族一起用餐，而且还要五十名衣着华丽的卫士陪侍在身旁。

约翰国王听说了修道院院长的生活方式，便打定主意加以制止。于是，他派人把老院长叫来见他。

"我的修道院院长，"国王说。"听说你住的房子比我的还要阔气很多，你好大的胆子！难道你不知道不允许有人比国王生活得还要好吗？这绝对不允许！"

"啊，国王陛下！"修道院院长说，"我花的都是自己的钱，我只是想让我的朋友和勇士们过得开心快乐，除此之外别无他意，请陛下不要误会！"

"我误会了你？"国王说。"这怎么可能？这偌大国土上的一切都归我所有，你竟然敢生活得比我好，你让

① abbot ['æbət] n. 男修道院院长

shame by living in grander style than I? One would think that you were trying to be king in my place."

"Oh, do not say so!" said the abbot "For I"—

"Not another word!" cried the king. "Your fault is **plain**①, and unless you can answer me three questions, your head shall be cut off, and all your riches shall be mine."

"I will try to answer them, O king!" said the abbot.

"Well, then," said King John, "as I sit here with my crown of gold on my head, you must tell me to within a day just how long I shall live. Secondly, you must tell me how soon I shall ride round the whole world; and lastly, you shall tell me what I think."

"O king!" said the abbot, "these are deep, hard questions, and I cannot answer them just now. But if you will give me two weeks to think about them, I will do the best that I can."

"Two weeks you shall have," said the king; "but if then you fail to answer me, you shall lose your head, and all your lands shall be mine."

The abbot went away very sad and in great fear. He first rode to Oxford. Here was a great school, called a university, and he wanted to see if any of the wise professors could help him. But they shook their heads, and said that there was nothing about King John in any of their books.

Then the abbot rode down to Cambridge, where there was another university. But not one of the teachers in that great school could help him.

At last, sad and **sorrowful**②, he rode toward home to **bid** his friends and his brave knights **goodbye**③. For now he had not a week to live.

II. THE THREE ANSWERS.

As the abbot was riding up the lane which led to his grand house, he met his **shepherd**④ going to the fields.

"Welcome home, good master!" cried the shepherd. "What news do you bring us from great King John?"

① plain [pleɪn] *a.* 清晰的，明显的

② sorrowful ['sɔrəfuəl; 'sɔː-] *a.* 充满悲伤的

③ bid sb. goodbye 向……告别

④ shepherd ['ʃepəd] *n.* 牧羊人

我的脸面往哪里搁？别人心里也许会想，这个家伙是不是想取代我做国王。"

"啊，陛下千万不能这样讲！"修道院院长说："我……"

"住口！"国王叫道。"你罪行昭彰，不需要再辩解。我要问你三个问题，如果你答不上来，你的脑袋就要搬家，你的所有财产也将归我所有。"

"陛下，我一定好好回答您的问题！"修道院院长说。

"那好！"约翰国王说，"现在我头戴金冠坐在这里，你要告诉我我能活多少岁，差一天也不行。第二个问题，如果我想骑马环游世界，告诉我要花多长时间。第三个问题，告诉我我心里想的是什么。"

"陛下！"修道院院长说，"这些问题实在太难太深奥了，我现在回答不上来。如果能给我两周时间考虑，我一定可以回答上来。"

"那就给你两周时间。"国王说，"如果再回答不上来，不光你的脑袋要搬家，你的所有土地都要归我所有。"

修道院院长离开的时候，心里感到既难过又害怕。他先骑马来到牛津，这里有一所伟大的大学，院长想或许能找到一位聪明的教授给予他帮助。可是教授们都直摇头，说书本里面根本找不到关于约翰国王的内容。

接着修道院院长又骑马去了剑桥，想得到剑桥大学老师们的帮助，可也是失望而归。

修道院院长的心情变得十分沉重，准备回家跟朋友和勇士们道别。当时剩下的时间已经不足一周了。

（2）三个答案

回家的路上，修道院院长遇见了正要下地干活的牧羊人。

"我的主人，您回来了！"牧羊人叫道。"您从约翰国王那里带回了什么消息？"

"Sad news, sad news," said the abbot; and then he told him all that had happened.

"Cheer up, cheer up, good master," said the shepherd. "Have you never yet heard that a fool may teach a wise man **wit**①? I think I can help you out of your trouble."

"You help me!" cried the abbot "How? how?"

"Well," answered the shepherd, "you know that everybody says that I look just like you, and that I have sometimes been mistaken for you. So, lend me your servants and your horse and your gown, and I will go up to London and see the king. If nothing else can be done, I can at least die in your place."

"My good shepherd," said the abbot, "you are very, very kind; and I have a mind to let you try your plan. But if the worst comes to the worst, you shall not die for me. I will die for myself."

So the shepherd got ready to go at once. He dressed himself with great care. Over his shepherd's coat he threw the abbot's long gown, and he borrowed the abbot's cap and golden staff. When all was ready, no one in the world would have thought that he was not the great man himself. Then he mounted his horse, and with a great train of servants set out for London.

Of course the king did not know him.

"Welcome, Sir Abbot!" he said. "It is a good thing that you have come back. But, **prompt**② as you are, if you fail to answer my three questions, you shall lose your head."

"I am ready to answer them, O king!" said the shepherd.

"Indeed, indeed!" said the king, and he laughed to himself. "Well, then, answer my first question: How long shall I live? Come, you must tell me to the very day."

"You shall live," said the shepherd, "until the day that you die, and not one day longer. And you shall die when you take your last breath, and not one moment before."

① wit [wit] *n.* 机智

② prompt [prɔmpt] *a.* 迅速的

"坏消息，糟糕的消息！"修道院院长说。接着，他就把事情的经过讲给了牧羊人听。

"振作起来，振作起来，我的主人，"牧师说，"您听没听说过愚笨的人也可以给聪明人传授智慧？这个问题就包在我身上了。"

"你能帮我？"修道院院长大喊了起来，"你快说怎么帮？怎么帮？"

"好，"牧羊人回答道，"您知道大家都说我长得十分像您，有时候还有人把我们俩认错。那何不让我借用您的佣人、马和衣服去伦敦见国王，大不了我替您掉脑袋。"

"我好心的牧羊人，"修道院院长说，"你的心实在太好了！我倒想让你试一试，不过即使这样不行，我也不会让你为我送死，我会自己去受死的。"

于是，牧羊人做好准备马上出发。他用修道院院长的长袍遮住牧羊穿的短衣，又借来他的帽子和首饰细心地装扮起来。一切收拾妥当后，恐怕世上没人能看出他是修道院院长的替身了。牧羊人骑着马，领着一帮仆人，浩浩荡荡地启程前往伦敦。

果然不出所料，国王并没有认出他是谁。

"欢迎，尊敬的修道院院长！"国王说，"欢迎回来。不过尽管你回来得很快，如果你回答不上我问的三个问题，你的脑袋还是要搬家。"

"啊，国王陛下，我已经做好准备了！"牧羊人说。

"那太好了！"国王说完大笑了起来。"那好，第一个问题：我究竟能活多长时间？快告诉我，我能活到哪一天。"

"陛下，"牧羊人说，"您能活到您去世的那一天，一天也不会多。您咽下最后一口气就要离开人世，一秒钟也不会早。"

"You shall live until the day that you die."

The king laughed.

"You are witty, I see," he said. "But we will let that pass, and say that your answer is right. And now tell me how soon I may ride round the world."

"You must rise with the sun," said the shepherd, "and you must ride with the sun until it rises again the next morning. As soon as you do that, you will find that you have ridden round the world in twenty-four hours."

The king laughed again. "Indeed," he said, "I did not think that it could be done so soon. You are not only witty, but you are wise, and we will let this answer pass. And now comes my third and last question: What do I think?"

"That is an easy question," said the shepherd. "You think that I am the Abbot of Canterbury. But, to tell you the truth, I am only his poor shepherd, and I have come to beg your pardon for him and for me." And with that, he threw off his long gown.

"您能活到您去世的那一天。"

国王笑了起来。

"你很机智。"国王说,"好吧,第一个问题就算你答对了。现在你告诉我,如果我骑马绕世界一周,需要花费多长时间。"

"如果太阳出来您就出发,"牧羊人说,"骑着马跟太阳一起走,直到第二天太阳再次升起,这时候您就会发现自己二十四小时内绕了世界一周。"

国王又笑了。"回答得极是!"国王说,"没想到你回答得这么快!你不但机智,而且聪明,这个答案也算通过了。现在我要问第三个问题,也是最后一个问题:我心里面想着什么?"

"这个问题简单。"牧羊人说,"陛下在想,我肯定是坎特伯雷修道院的院长。可实话禀告陛下,我只是他的穷牧人,到这儿来是求您对我们俩开恩的。"说完,

· 039 ·

The king laughed loud and long.

"A merry fellow you are," said he, "and you shall be the Abbot of Canterbury in your master's place."

"O king! that cannot be," said the shepherd; "for I can neither read nor write."

"Very well, then," said the king, "I will give you something else to pay you for this merry joke. I will give you four pieces of silver every week as long as you live. And when you get home, you may tell the old abbot that you have brought him a free pardon from King John."

牧羊人脱下了他身上的长袍。

国王放声大笑了好一阵儿。

"你这个家伙真讨人喜欢。"国王说,"应该让你来做坎特伯雷修道院的院长。"

"啊,陛下!那可使不得。"牧师说道,"我不识字,也不会写字。"

"既然这样,那好吧!"国王说,"为了这个有趣的玩笑,我准备额外犒赏你。从现在开始在你有生之年,每周都可以从我这里得到四块银币。回去后你告诉修道院老院长,就说约翰国王看在你的分上已经宽恕了他。"

7. A Story of Robin Hood

In the rude days of King Richard and King John there were many great woods in England. The most famous of these was Sherwood forest, where the king often went to hunt deer. In this forest there lived a band of **daring**① men called **outlaws**②.

They had done something that was against the laws of the land, and had been forced to hide themselves in the woods to save their lives. There they spent their time in roaming about among the trees, in hunting the king's deer, and in robbing rich travelers that came that way.

There were nearly a hundred of these outlaws, and their leader was a bold fellow called Robin Hood. They were dressed in suits of green, and armed with bows and arrows; and sometimes they carried long wooden **lances**③ and broadswords, which they knew how to handle well. Whenever they had taken anything, it was brought and laid at the feet of Robin Hood, whom they called their king. He then divided it fairly among them, giving to each man his just share.

Robin never allowed his men to harm anybody but the rich men who lived in great houses and did no work. He was always kind to the poor, and he often sent help to them; and for that reason the common people looked upon him as their friend.

7. 罗宾汉的故事

① daring ['dɛəriŋ] *a.* 大胆的
② outlaw ['autlɔː] *n.* 逃犯

③ lance [læns] *n.* 长矛

　　很久以前，在理查国王和约翰国王统治时期，英格兰有很多大森林，最有名的要数舍伍德森林。那里不仅是国王的狩猎地，而且还住着一群被称为"逃犯"的胆大包天的家伙。

　　由于犯了法，为了逃命这些人只好藏身林中四处游窜。他们有时去偷猎国王的鹿，有时还会去抢劫过路的有钱人。

　　这些"逃犯"大约有一百人，领头的是一个叫罗宾汉的胆大家伙。他们身穿绿装，手拿弓箭，有时还带着大刀和木制长矛，对于这些武器他们样样精通。无论什么时候，只要一有收获，他们都会拿去交给首领罗宾汉，让他来公平地分给大家，每人都能分到各自应得的一份。

　　罗宾汉严禁手下人祸害穷苦百姓，他们的目标是那些住在豪宅里面不劳而获的有钱人。对待穷苦百姓，罗宾汉非常友善，时不时还接济他们一下。因此，老百姓都把他看成自己的朋友。

Long after he was dead, men liked to talk about his deeds. Some praised him, and some blamed him. He was, indeed, a rude, lawless fellow; but at that time, people did not think of right and wrong as they do now.

A great many songs were made up about Robin Hood, and these songs were sung in the cottages and huts all over the land for hundreds of years afterward.

Here is a little story that is told in one of those songs:—

Robin Hood was standing one day under a green tree by the roadside. While he was listening to the birds among the leaves, he saw a young man passing by. This young man was dressed in a fine suit of bright red cloth; and, as he tripped gaily along the road, he seemed to be as happy as the day.

"I will not trouble him," said Robin Hood, "for I think he is on his way to his wedding."

The next day Robin stood in the same place. He had not been there long when he saw the same young man coming down the road. But he did not seem to be so happy this time. He had left his **scarlet**[①] coat at home, and at every step he sighed and **groaned**[②].

"Ah the sad day! the sad day!" he kept saying to himself.

Then Robin Hood stepped out from under the tree, and said,—

"I say, young man! Have you any money to spare for my merry men and me?"

"I have nothing at all," said the young man, "but five **shillings**[③] and a ring."

"A gold ring?" asked Robin.

"Yes," said the young man, "it is a gold ring. Here it is."

"Ah, I see!" said Robin; "it is a wedding ring."

"I have kept it these seven years," said the young man; "I have kept it to give to my bride on our wedding day. We were going to be married yesterday. But her father has promised her to a rich old man whom she never saw. And now my heart is broken."

即便去世后很多年，罗宾汉的故事依然在人们中间流传着。有人赞他，有人谤他，而他其实只是一个举止粗鲁、目无法纪的家伙。可是在当时那个年代，人们对于孰是孰非的观念跟现在不同。

有许许多多歌唱罗宾汉的歌曲，数百年来一直在民间传唱。

下面这个小故事就来自其中的一首歌：

有一天，罗宾汉站在路边的大树下听鸟儿歌唱，忽然他看见一个穿着红色套装的年轻人，迈着轻盈的脚步走了过来，心情好得就像当日晴朗的天空一样。

"我不去打扰他。"罗宾汉说，"我猜今天一定是小伙子的大喜之日。"

第二天，罗宾汉又站在原处。没过多久，他又看见那个年轻人从这里经过，不过好像这次他的心情不太好。小伙子没有穿那件红色外套，一边走，一边低声叹息着。

"唉，多么让人伤心的一天！多么让人伤心的一天！"小伙子不停地自言自语道。

罗宾汉从树下面走了出去，说："我说，年轻人！你有没有钱给我和我的弟兄们花？"

"我什么都没有，"年轻人说，"只有五个先令和一枚戒指。"

"戒指是金子的吗？"罗宾汉问。

"是的，"年轻人说，"是金戒指，你要的话就拿去！"

"啊，我明白了！"罗宾汉说道，"这是一枚结婚戒指。"

"七年了，我一直保存着这枚戒指。"年轻人说，"就想在结婚的那一天把它送给我的新娘。我们原本打算昨天举行婚礼，可是女孩的父亲硬要把她嫁给一个不认识的有钱老头子，现在我的心都要碎了。"

① scarlet [skɑːlət] a. 猩红色的
② groan [grəun] v. 呻吟

③ shilling ['ʃiliŋ] n. 先令

"What is your name?" asked Robin.

"My name is Allin-a-Dale," said the young man.

"What will you give me, in gold or fee," said Robin, "if I will help you win your bride again in spite of the rich old man to whom she has been promised?"

"I have no money," said Allin, "but I will promise to be your servant."

"How many miles is it to the place where the maiden lives?" asked Robin.

"It is not far," said Allin. "But she is to be married this very day, and the church is five miles away."

Then Robin made haste to dress himself as a **harper**①; and in the afternoon he stood in the door of the church.

"Who are you?" said the **bishop**②, "and what are you doing here?"

"I am a bold harper," said Robin, "the best in the north country."

"I am glad you have come," said the bishop kindly. "There is no music that I like so well as that of the harp. Come in, and play for us."

"I will go in," said Robin Hood; "but I will not give you any music until I see

"你叫什么名字?"罗宾汉问。

"我叫阿林·戴尔。"年轻人回答说。

"要是我能帮你把新娘从老头那里夺回来,"罗宾汉说,"你打算怎么报答我,给我金子还是给我酬金?"

"我身无分文,"阿林说,"不过我可以做你的仆人。"

"那个女孩住在离这里多远的地方?"罗宾汉问。

"不远。"阿林答道,"但她今天就要嫁人了,举行婚礼的教堂离这里有五英里。"

罗宾汉赶忙把自己打扮成竖琴师的模样,下午时分来到教堂的门前。

"你是谁?"主教问他,"来这里有何贵干?"

"我是一个勇敢的竖琴师,"罗宾汉说,"是北方最好的竖琴师。"

"你能来我很高兴,"主教和善地说,"所有的音乐里面,我最喜欢竖琴弹的曲子。快进来给我们演奏吧!"

① harper ['hɑːpə] n. 竖琴师
② bishop ['biʃəp] n. 主教

the bride and bridegroom."

Just then an old man came in. He was dressed in rich clothing, but was bent with age, and was **feeble**[①] and gray. By his side walked a fair young girl. Her cheeks were very pale, and her eyes were full of tears.

"This is no match," said Robin. "Let the bride choose for herself."

Then he put his horn to his lips, and blew three times. The very next minute, four and twenty men, all dressed in green, and carrying long bows in their hands, came running across the fields. And as they marched into the church, all in a row, the foremost among them was Allin-a-Dale.

"Now whom do you choose?" said Robin to the maiden.

"I choose Allin-a-Dale," she said, blushing.

"And Allin-a-Dale you shall have," said Robin; "and he that takes you from Allin-a-Dale shall find that he has Robin Hood to deal with."

And so the fair maiden and Allin-a-Dale were married then and there, and the rich old man went home in a great rage.

> *"And thus having ended this merry wedding,*
> *The bride looked like a queen:*
> *And so they returned to the merry green wood,*
> *Amongst the leaves so green."*

① feeble ['fi:bl] a. 虚弱的

"我当然会进去。"罗宾汉说,"不过,我要看到新郎新娘再演奏。"

就在这时,一个衣着华贵的老头走了进来。他年老体衰,驼着背,满头白发,身旁走着一位年轻貌美的姑娘。这个姑娘脸色苍白,眼中噙满泪水。

"他们根本就不般配。"罗宾汉说,"为什么不让新娘自己挑选新郎?"

说完,罗宾汉吹响了三声号角。顷刻间,二十四名身穿绿装的男子出现在田野中,他们手持长弓冲进教堂,阿林·戴尔走在队伍的最前面。

"如果现在让你选新郎,你愿意选谁?"罗宾汉向少女问道。

"我选阿林·戴尔。"姑娘羞红着脸说。

"那就如你所愿。"罗宾汉说,"如果今后有人胆敢把你从阿林·戴尔身边抢走,就说我罗宾汉不答应。"

于是,美丽的姑娘和阿林·戴尔在教堂里喜结连理,只剩下那个有钱的老头气急败坏地回家去了。

"愉快的婚礼结束,
美丽的新娘貌若女王;
返回快乐的绿林时他们结伴,
消失在枝叶茂盛的丛林间。"

8. Bruce and the Spider

There was once a king of Scotland whose name was Robert Bruce. He had need to be both brave and wise, for the times in which he lived were wild and rude. The King of England was at war with him, and had led a great army into Scotland to drive him out of the land.

Battle after battle had been fought. Six times had Bruce led his brave little army against his foes; and six times had his men been beaten, and driven into flight. At last his army was scattered, and he was forced to hide himself in the woods and in lonely places among the mountains.

One rainy day, Bruce lay on the ground under a rude shed, listening to the **patter**[1] of the drops on the roof above him. He was tired and sick at heart, and ready to give up all hope. It seemed to him that there was no use for him to try to do anything more.

As he lay thinking, he saw a spider over his head, making ready to **weave**[2] her web. He watched her as she **toiled**[3] slowly and with great care. Six times she tried to throw her **frail**[4] **thread**[5] from one **beam**[6] to another, and six times it fell short.

"Poor thing!" said Bruce: "you, too, know what it is to fail."

But the spider did not lose hope with the sixth failure. With still more care,

8. 布鲁斯国王和蜘蛛

　　从前，有一位苏格兰国王名叫罗伯特·布鲁斯。身处当时那个既蛮荒又残酷的时代，国王必须要智勇双全。当时，英格兰国王正率领大军攻打苏格兰，企图将布鲁斯国王赶出国门。

　　战争打了一场又一场，布鲁斯带领自己的精锐部队与敌人展开了六次激战，结果都被打得落荒而逃。最后他的人马都被打散了，自己也被迫躲进荒凉的山林之中。

　　一个下雨天，布鲁斯藏身于一个简陋的小棚子里，躺在地上听着屋顶上滴滴答答的雨声。当时他感到身心疲惫，已经准备好要放弃一切希望，因为对他而言，似乎所有的努力都是徒劳无益的。

　　就在布鲁斯躺在那里寻思的时候，正好发现头顶上有一只蜘蛛准备吐丝织网，他目不转睛地注视着这个小家伙，看着它缓慢而小心地忙碌着。整整六次，蜘蛛想要把脆弱的蛛丝从这边的横梁结到那边的横梁上，可是每次都失败了。

　　"可怜的家伙！"布鲁斯说，"你也品尝到失败的滋味了吧！"

　　然而蜘蛛并没有放弃希望，依然小心翼翼地准备进

① patter ['pætə] *n.* 嗒嗒声

② weave [wi:v] *v.* 编织
③ toil [tɔil] *v.* 辛勤劳动
④ frail [freil] *a.* 脆弱的
⑤ thread [θred] *n.* 线
⑥ beam [bi:m] *n.* 横梁

· 051 ·

she made ready to try for the seventh time. Bruce almost forgot his own troubles as he watched her swing herself out upon the **slender**① line. Would she fail again? No! The thread was carried safely to the beam, and fastened there.

"I, too, will try a seventh time!" cried Bruce.

He arose and called his men together. He told them of his plans, and sent them out with messages of cheer to his disheartened people. Soon there was an army of brave Scotch-men around him. Another battle was fought, and the King of England was glad to go back into his own country.

I have heard it said, that, after that day, no one by the name of Bruce would ever hurt a spider. The lesson which the little creature had taught the king was never forgotten.

① slender ['slendə] *a.* 细长的

行第七次的努力。布鲁斯注视着蜘蛛在纤细的蛛丝①上摇晃着身躯,几乎把自己所有的烦恼忘到了九霄云外。这次它还会失败吗?不!蛛丝终于稳稳地结到了横梁上,固定在那里。

"我也要做第七次努力!"布鲁斯大叫了起来。

他一跃而起,重新召集起自己的人马。布鲁斯把自己的计划讲给手下听,还把这个鼓舞人心的故事告诉那些已经失去信心的人们。很快,他的身边又聚集起一群勇敢的苏格兰人。战争再一次打响了,他们终于把英格兰国王赶回了老家。

听人们说从那以后,凡是名字叫布鲁斯的人都不会伤害蜘蛛。人们将永远铭记这个小东西给国王上的那一课。

9. The Black Douglas

In Scotland, in the time of King Robert Bruce, there lived a brave man whose name was Douglas. His hair and beard were black and long, and his face was **tanned**① and dark; and for this reason people nicknamed him the Black Douglas. He was a good friend of the king, and one of his strongest helpers.

In the war with the English, who were trying to drive Bruce from Scotland, the Black Douglas did many brave deeds; and the English people became very much afraid of him. By and by the fear of him spread all through the land. Nothing could frighten an English lad more than to tell him that the Black Douglas was not far away. Women would tell their children, when they were naughty, that the Black Douglas would get them; and this would make them very quiet and good.

There was a large castle in Scotland which the English had taken early in the war. The Scottish soldiers wanted very much to take it again, and the Black Douglas and his men went one day to see what they could do. It happened to be a holiday, and most of the English soldiers in the castle were eating and drinking and having a merry time. But they had left watchmen on the wall to see that the Scottish soldiers did not come upon them **unawares**②; and so they felt quite safe.

In the evening, when it was growing dark, the wife of one of the soldiers

9. 黑面人道格拉斯

① tanned [tænd] a. 被晒成褐色的

② unawares [ˌʌnəˈwɛəz] ad. 出其不意地

　　在罗伯特·布鲁斯国王的统治时期，有一个苏格兰勇士名叫道格拉斯。此人的头发和胡须又黑又长，再加上晒得面色黝黑，人们便给他起了绰号叫"黑面人道格拉斯"。道格拉斯是国王的好朋友，而且也是国王的得力助手。

　　在英格兰和苏格兰之间的那场战争中，英格兰人企图把布鲁斯国王赶走，"黑面人道格拉斯"为苏格兰立下了赫赫战功，英格兰人只要一提起道格拉斯，就会感到不寒而栗。慢慢地，人们对道格拉斯的恐惧传遍了整个英格兰，英格兰人吓唬小孩的最好办法莫过于说"黑面人道格拉斯"要来了。因此，只要谁家的小孩调皮捣蛋，妇女们就会吓唬他们说"黑面人道格拉斯"要来把他们抓走。只要这样，孩子们马上就会变得既安静又听话。

　　战争初期，英格兰人占领了一座巨大的苏格兰城堡，苏格兰士兵日夜盘算着要把它夺回去。一天，"黑面人道格拉斯"带领部下前去侦察。那天碰巧是节日，大多数英格兰士兵都待在城堡里面饮酒作乐。为了防止苏格兰人的偷袭，英格兰人还专门安排哨兵到城墙上瞭望，因此他们觉得十分安全。

　　当天晚上，夜色慢慢降临。一个英格兰士兵的妻

Fifty Famous Stories Retold

went up on the wall with her child in her arms. As she looked over into the fields below the castle, she saw some dark objects moving toward the foot of the wall. In the dusk she could not make out what they were, and so she pointed them out to one of the watchmen.

"Pooh, pooh!" said the watchman. "Those are nothing to frighten us. They are the farmer's cattle, trying to find their way home. The farmer himself is enjoying the holiday, and he has forgotten to bring them in. If the Douglas should happen this way before morning, he will be sorry for his carelessness."

But the dark objects were not cattle. They were the Black Douglas and his men, **creeping**① on hands and feet toward the foot of the castle wall. Some of them were dragging ladders behind them through the grass. They would soon be climbing to the top of the wall. None of the English soldiers dreamed that they were within many miles of the place.

The woman watched them until the last one had passed around a corner out of sight. She was not afraid, for in the darkening **twilight**② they looked indeed like cattle. After a little while she began to sing to her child:—

> *"Hush ye, hush ye, little pet ye,*
> *Hush ye, hush ye, do not fret ye,*
> *The Black Douglas shall not get ye."*

All at once a **gruff**③ voice was heard behind her, saying, "Don't be so sure about that!"

She looked around, and there stood the Black Douglas himself. At the same moment a Scottish soldier climbed off a ladder and leaped upon the wall; and then there came another and another and another, until the wall was covered with them. Soon there was hot fighting in every part of the castle. But the English were so taken by surprise that they could not do much. Many of them were killed, and in a little while the Black Douglas and his men were the masters of the castle, which by right belonged to them.

子抱着孩子走到城墙上面，往城外的田野里眺望，发现一些黑影正在向城墙方向移动。由于天色已晚，她看不清那些黑影到底是什么东西，便指给一个哨兵看。

"呸，呸！"哨兵说，"有什么可大惊小怪的！那是农夫的牛群，它们正赶着往家走。农夫自己待在家里过节，把牛忘在外面了。如果'黑面人道格拉斯'真的天亮前来，那农夫一定会为自己的大意感到后悔的！"

可实际上那些黑影并不是牛群，而是"黑面人道格拉斯"和他的部下，他们正从草地上朝城墙方向爬行着，有的人身后还拖着梯子，他们马上就要登上城墙。英格兰士兵做梦也不会想到，敌人已经在他们的眼皮子底下。

那个妇女站在那里看着，一直到最后一个黑影拐了个弯不见了。她并没有感到害怕，因为在渐深的暮色中，那些影子看起来真的很像牛。过了一会儿，她哼起了歌谣：

"小宝贝，不要吵啊，不要吵，
小宝贝，不要闹啊，不要闹，
'黑面人道格拉斯'不会来到。"

突然，一个粗哑的声音从她身后传来，说："那可不一定！"

那个妇女转身一看，发现此人正是"黑面人道格拉斯"。几乎与此同时，一个苏格兰士兵从梯子上爬上来，一跃跳上城墙；紧接着一个又一个苏格兰士兵站满了城墙。很快，城堡里面展开了激烈的战斗。英格兰人在吃惊之余根本无力抵抗，伤亡惨重。没用多长时间，"黑面人道格拉斯"和他的部下就夺回了本就属于他们的城堡。

---

① creep [kri:p] v. 匍匐

② twilight ['twailait] n. 暮色

③ gruff [grʌf] a. 粗暴的

"Don't be so sure about that!"

As for the woman and her child, the Black Douglas would not suffer any one to harm them. After a while they went back to England; and whether the mother made up any more songs about the Black Douglas I cannot tell.

"那可不一定！"

至于那个妇女和她的小孩，"黑面人道格拉斯"没有让任何人伤害他们。不久以后，母子两人返回了英格兰。那个母亲到底有没有再编有关"黑面人道格拉斯"的歌谣，我便不得而知了。

10. Three Men of Gotham

There is a town in England called Gotham, and many merry stories are told of the **queer**① people who used to live there.

One day two men of Gotham met on a bridge. Hodge was coming from the market, and Peter was going to the market.

"Where are you going?" said Hodge.

"I am going to the market to buy sheep," said Peter.

"Buy sheep?" said Hodge. "And which way will you bring them home?"

"I shall bring them over this bridge," said Peter.

"No, you shall not," said Hodge.

"Yes, but I will," said Peter.

"You shall not," said Hodge.

"I will," said Peter.

Then they beat with their sticks on the ground as though there had been a hundred sheep between them.

"Take care!" cried Peter. "Look out that my sheep don't jump on the bridge."

"I care not where they jump," said Hodge; "but they shall not go over it."

"But they shall," said Peter.

10. 三个哥坦人

① queer [kwiə] *a.* 异乎寻常的

英格兰有一个名叫哥坦的城市，那里生活着一些稀奇古怪的人，有许许多多关于他们的有趣故事。

一天，两个哥坦城的人在桥上相遇。原来是赫奇从集市上返回，而彼得正好要去那里。

"你要到哪里去？"赫奇问。

"我要去集市买羊。"彼得回答。

"买羊？"赫奇说，"那你准备把羊从哪条路带回家？"

"从这座桥上带回去。"彼得说。

"不行，你不能从这里过。"赫奇说。

"我就要从这儿过。"彼得说。

"不准你从这儿过！"赫奇说。

"我就要过！"彼得又说。

说着说着，他们开始用手杖敲打着桥面，就好像真的有一百只羊从那里经过似的。

"当心！"彼得叫了起来，"注意别让我的羊在桥上乱跳。"

"我才不管它们在哪儿跳，"赫奇说，"我不许羊从桥上过去。"

"偏要让它们从这里过去。"彼得说。

"Have a care," said Hodge; "for if you say too much, I will put my fingers in your mouth."

"Will you?" said Peter.

Just then another man of Gotham came from the market with a **sack**① of **meal**② on his horse. He heard his neighbors quarreling about sheep; but he could see no sheep between them, and so he stopped and spoke to them.

"Ah, you foolish fellows!" he cried. "It is strange that you will never learn wisdom. — Come here, Peter, and help me lay my sack on my shoulder."

Peter did so, and the man carried his meal to the side of the bridge.

"Now look at me," he said, "and learn a lesson." And he opened the mouth of the sack, and poured all the meal into the river.

"Now, neighbors," he said, "can you tell how much meal is in my sack?"

"How much meal is in my sack?"

① sack [sæk] *n.* 大口袋
② meal [mi:l] *n.* 粗磨面粉

"当心！"赫奇说，"你再啰唆，我就要把手指头塞进你的嘴里。"

"你敢！"彼得回敬道。

恰好当时另一个哥坦城的人牵着马从集市上返回，马背上驮着一袋面粉。此人听见邻居们正在为羊的事情争吵，可是他一只羊也没看见！于是他停下脚步，开口对那两个人说话。

"喂，你们两个蠢蛋！"此人叫道，"真奇怪，你们怎么就是不能学聪明一点？彼得过来，帮我把袋子放到肩膀上。"

彼得照做了，然后那个人又把面粉扛到桥边。

"现在看着我，"此人又说，"我要给你们一个教训！"说完他打开口袋，把面粉全部倒进了河里。

"现在，邻居们，"他问，"谁能告诉我袋子里还剩下多少面粉？"

"袋子里还剩下多少面粉？"

"There is none at all!" cried Hodge and Peter together.

"You are right," said the man; "and you that stand here and quarrel about nothing, have no more sense in your heads than I have meal in my sack!"

"一点面粉都没有了！"赫奇和彼得一起叫道。

"你们说对了。"这个人说，"你们站在这里为不存在的东西争吵，你们的脑袋就像这个口袋一样，空空如也！"

11. Other Wise Men of Gotham

One day, news was brought to Gotham that the king was coming that way, and that he would pass through the town. This did not please the men of Gotham at all. They hated the king, for they knew that he was a cruel, bad man. If he came to their town, they would have to find food and lodging for him and his men; and if he saw anything that pleased him, he would be sure to take it for his own. What should they do?

They met together to talk the matter over.

"Let us **chop**[①] down the big trees in the woods, so that they will block up all the roads that lead into the town," said one of the wise men.

"Good!" said all the rest.

So they went out with their axes, and soon all the roads and paths to the town were filled with **logs**[②] and **brush**[③]. The king's horse-men would have a hard time of it getting into Gotham. They would either have to make a new road, or give up the plan altogether, and go on to some other place.

When the king came, and saw that the road had been blocked up, he was very angry.

"Who chopped those trees down in my way?" he asked of two country lads that were passing by.

"The men of Gotham," said the lads.

11. 哥坦城其他的聪明人

　　一天，有消息传到哥坦城，说国王很快要从这里经过。得到消息的哥坦城的人一点也高兴不起来。他们憎恨国王，因为大家都知道国王是一个残暴的恶人。如果国王来到这里，哥坦城的人就要给他和一起随行的人准备膳食和住宿，而且凡是国王喜欢的东西，就一定要据为己有。他们该怎么办呢？

　　于是，哥坦城的人聚在一起商量这件事情。

　　"我们把树林里的大树砍倒，堵住所有通向城里的道路。"一个聪明人说。

　　"这个主意好！"其他人附和道。

　　于是，他们带着斧头出发了。很快，所有通往城里的道路都被木头和树枝堵住了。国王的马队要进哥坦城将会十分困难，他们要么需要开辟一条新路，要么就得放弃原来的计划到别处去。

　　国王看见道路都被堵死了，便十分生气。

　　"是谁砍倒这些树挡住了我的路？"国王询问两个经过的乡下小孩。

　　"是哥坦人。"小孩们说。

① chop [tʃɒp] v. 砍

② log [lɒg] n. 木材
③ brush [brʌʃ] n. 断落（或砍下）的树枝

· 067 ·

"Well," said the king, "go and tell the men of Gotham that I shall send my **sheriff**① into their town, and have all their noses cut off."

The two lads ran to the town as fast as they could, and made known what the king had said.

Everybody was in great fright. The men ran from house to house, carrying the news, and asking one another what they should do.

"Our wits have kept the king out of the town," said one; "and so now our wits must save our noses."

"True, true!" said the others. "But what shall we do?"

Then one, whose name was Dobbin, and who was thought to be the wisest of them all, said, "Let me tell you something. Many a man has been punished because he was wise, but I have never heard of any one being harmed because he was a fool. So, when the king's sheriff comes, let us all act like fools."

"Good, good!" cried the others. "We will all act like fools."

It was no easy thing for the king's men to open the roads; and while they were doing it, the king grew tired of waiting, and went back to London. But very early one morning, the sheriff with a party of fierce soldiers rode through the woods, and between the fields, toward Gotham. Just before they reached the town, they saw a queer sight. The old men were rolling big stones up the hill, and all the young men were looking on, and **grunting**② very loudly.

The sheriff stopped his horses, and asked what they were doing.

"We are rolling stones uphill to make the sun rise," said one of the old men.

"You foolish fellow!" said the sheriff. "Don't you know that the sun will rise without any help?"

"Ah! will it?" said the old man. "Well, I never thought of that. How wise you are!"

"And what are you doing?" said the sheriff to the young men.

① sheriff ['ʃerif] n. 郡长

② grunt [grʌnt] v. 发哼声

"好啊！"国王说，"你们去告诉哥坦人，就说我要派郡长来把他们的鼻子割掉。"

两个小孩吓得拼命跑回城里，把国王的话转告给了大家。

哥坦城的人个个都感到十分恐惧。人们挨家挨户奔走相告，都不知道该怎么应对。

"既然我们能够用智慧阻止国王进城，"有个人说，"现在我们就要用智慧来挽救我们的鼻子。"

"就是！就是！"其他人附和说，"那我们该怎么做呢？"

这时，他们当中被公认为最聪明的人多宾说："我想让大家明白，很多人都是因为太聪明才遭受到惩罚，可是我还没听说过有人因为愚蠢而受到伤害的。所以国王的郡长来后，我们大家都要装成傻瓜。

"好主意！好主意！"其他人都叫了起来，"我们都装成傻瓜。"

要打通进城的道路绝非易事。国王的部下还没把路开完，国王已经等得不耐烦返回伦敦去了。一天清晨，郡长带着人马气势汹汹地穿过树林，从田野里径直向哥坦城赶来。快到城里的时候，他们见到一副奇怪的景象：老人们正在把大石头往山上推，年轻人却站在一边袖手旁观，嘴里还在大声呻吟着。

郡长勒住马，问这些人在干什么。

"我们把石头往山上推，好让太阳升起来。"一个老人回答说。

"你们这群傻瓜！"郡长说，"难道你们不知道太阳无须借助任何力量，自然就会升起吗？"

"啊，真的吗？"那个老人说，"太好了，我们怎么从来没有想到过。你真聪明啊！"

"那你们又在做什么呢？"郡长又问那些年轻人。

Fifty Famous Stories Retold

"Oh, we do the grunting while our fathers do the working," they answered.

"I see," said the sheriff. "Well, that is the way the world goes everywhere."

And he rode on toward the town.

He soon came to a field where a number of men were building a stone wall.

"What are you doing?" he asked.

"**Why**[①], master," they answered, "there is a **cuckoo**[②] in this field, and we are building a wall around it so as to keep the bird from **straying away**[③]."

"You foolish fellows!" said the sheriff. "Don't you know that the bird will fly over the top of your wall, no matter how high you build it?"

"Why, no," they said. "We never thought of that. How very wise you are!"

The sheriff next met a man who was carrying a door on his back.

"What are you doing?" he asked.

"I have just started on a long journey," said the man.

"But why do you carry that door?" asked the sheriff.

"I left my money at home."

"Then why didn't you leave the door at home too?"

"I was afraid of thieves; and you see, if I have the door with me, they can't break it open and get in."

"You foolish fellow!" said the sheriff. "It would be safer to leave the door at home, and carry the money with you."

"Ah, would it, though?" said the man. "Now, I never thought of that. You are the wisest man that I ever saw."

Then the sheriff rode on with his men; but every one that they met was doing some silly thing.

"Truly. I believe that the people of Gotham are all fools," said one of the horsemen.

"That is true," said another. "It would be a shame to harm such simple people."

"噢，父辈们在忙碌，我们年轻人站在旁边哼哼。"他们回答道。

"我明白了。"郡长说，"很好，这种事情全世界都一样。"

说完，他继续往城里骑去。

很快，郡长走到一片田野，看见很多人正在修一道石墙。

"你们在做什么？"他又问。

"噢，长官，"他们答道，"田野里有一只杜鹃，我们想修一道墙围起来，这样它就跑不掉了。"

"你们这群傻瓜！"郡长说，"你们难道不知道不管墙砌得有多高，鸟都能从墙头上飞出去吗？"

"哎呀，不错。"他们说，"我们怎么从来没有想到过。你真聪明啊！"

接着，郡长又遇到一个人，此人的背上正扛着一扇门。

"你在干什么？"郡长问。

"我正要出一趟远门。"此人答道。

"那你为什么背着门？"郡长又问。

"我把钱留在家里了。"

"那你为什么不把门也留在家里呢？"

"我怕有贼偷！你看，如果我把门带在身边，贼就不能破门而入了。"

"你这个蠢货！"郡长说，"你应该把门留在家里，把钱带在身上，这样不是更安全吗？"

"啊，真是这样。"这个人说，"我居然没有想到这一点。你是我见过的最聪明的人。"

郡长和他的部下骑着马继续往前走，他们遇到的每一个人都在做着一些愚蠢的事情。

"真的，我敢肯定哥坦城的人都是些傻瓜。"一个骑兵说。

---

① why [hwai] *int.* 噢！
② cuckoo ['kuːkuː] *n.* 布谷鸟
③ stray away 走失

"Let us ride back to London, and tell the king all about them," said the sheriff.

"Yes, let us do so," said the horsemen.

So they went back, and told the king that Gotham was a town of fools; and the king laughed, and said that if that was the case, he would not harm them, but would let them keep their noses.

"一点也不错。"另一个骑兵说,"伤害那些蠢蛋可不是什么光彩的事。"

"我们回伦敦吧,把大家看到的禀告给国王。"郡长说。

"好吧,就这么办!"骑兵们说。

于是郡长和他的手下返回伦敦,告诉国王哥坦城是一个愚人城。国王听后便哈哈大笑起来,说如果果真如此,就不去伤害那些人了,就让他们留着自己的鼻子吧!

12. The Miller of the Dee

Once upon a time there lived on the banks of the River Dee a **miller**①, who was the happiest man in England. He was always busy from morning till night, and he was always singing as merrily as any **lark**②. He was so cheerful that he made everybody else cheerful; and people all over the land liked to talk about his pleasant ways. At last the king heard about him.

"I will go down and talk with this wonderful miller," he said. "Perhaps he can tell me how to be happy."

As soon as he stepped inside of the mill, he heard the miller singing:—

"I envy nobody—no, not I!—
For I am as happy as I can be;
And nobody envies me."

"You're wrong, my friend," said the king. "You're wrong as wrong can be. I envy you; and I would gladly change places with you, if I could only be as lighthearted as you are."

The miller smiled, and bowed to the king.

"I am sure I could not think of changing places with you, sir," he said.

"Now tell me," said the king, "what makes you so cheerful and glad here

12. 迪水河畔的磨坊主

① miller ['milə] *n.* 磨坊主

② lark [lɑːk] *n.* 百灵鸟

  从前，迪水河畔有一位磨坊主，是全英格兰最快乐的人。此人每天在磨坊里从早忙到晚，总像百灵鸟一样快乐地歌唱着。他不但自己快乐，还把快乐传递给其他人。大家对此常常津津乐道，最后竟然连国王也听说了他。
  "我要和这个神奇的磨坊主谈一谈。"国王说，"兴许他能告诉我快乐的秘诀。"
  国王刚走进磨坊，耳朵里就传来磨坊主的歌声：

  "我不羡慕别人，啊，我也不妒忌别人！
  我如此欢乐，
   也没有人会妒忌我。"

  "你唱得不对，我的朋友。"国王说，"你大错特错了，我就妒忌你。如果能像你一样无忧无虑地生活，我愿意拿王位和你交换。"
  磨坊主微笑着向国王鞠了一躬。
  "我怎敢和您交换王位，陛下！"磨坊主说。
  "那你现在告诉我，"国王说，"是什么让你在这满是灰尘的磨坊里也能如此快乐？我虽然贵为国王，却每

in your dusty mill, while I, who am king, am sad and in trouble every day."

The miller smiled again, and said, "I do not know why you are sad, but I can easily tell why I am glad. I earn my own bread; I love my wife and my children; I love my friends, and they love me; and I owe not a penny to any man. Why should I not be happy? For here is the River Dee, and every day it turns my mill; and the mill **grinds**① the corn that feeds my wife, my babes, and me."

"Say no more," said the king. "Stay where you are, and be happy still. But I envy you. Your dusty cap is worth more than my golden crown. Your mill does more for you than my kingdom can do for me. If there were more such men as you, what a good place this world would be! Goodbye, my friend!"

The king turned about, and walked sadly away; and the miller went back to his work singing:—

"Oh, I'm as happy as happy can be,
For I live by the side of the River Dee!"

天都在为烦恼忧愁而苦恼。"

　　磨坊主又笑了起来，说："也许我不懂得您为什么而忧愁，可我快乐的诀窍说起来却十分简单。我靠自己的双手养家糊口，爱自己的妻子和孩子，爱我的朋友，他们也爱我，我不欠别人一分钱。我为什么还要不快乐呢？在这里，每天迪水河水让机器转动，机器磨出来的粮食养活了我和我的家人。"

① grind [graind] v. 磨碎

　　"不要再说了。"国王说，"你继续在这里快乐吧！我羡慕你，你的帽子上虽然沾满了灰尘，可是它比我的金冠更宝贵，磨坊给予你的，整个王国也给不了我。如果有更多像你这样的人，这个世界将会变成一片乐土。再见了，我的朋友！"

　　说完，国王转过身失望地离去了。磨坊主又开始一边工作一边歌唱：

　　　　"啊！我是多么快乐呀！
　　　　因为我住在迪水河畔！"

13. Sir Philip Sidney

A cruel battle was being fought. The ground was covered with dead and dying men. The air was hot and **stifling**①. The sun shone down without pity on the wounded soldiers lying in the blood and dust.

One of these soldiers was a nobleman, whom everybody loved for his gentleness and kindness. Yet now he was no better off than the poorest man in the field. He had been wounded, and would die; and he was suffering much with pain and thirst.

When the battle was over, his friends hurried to his aid. A soldier came running with a cup in his hand.

"Here, Sir Philip," he said, "I have brought you some clear, cool water from the **brook**②. I will raise your head so that you can drink."

The cup was placed to Sir Philip's lips. How thankfully he looked at the man who had brought it! Then his eyes met those of a dying soldier who was lying on the ground close by. The **wistful**③ look in the poor man's face spoke plainer than words.

"Give the water to that man," said Sir Philip quickly; and then, pushing the cup toward him, he said, "Here, my comrade, take this. Thy need is greater than mine."

What a brave, noble man he was! The name of Sir Philip Sidney will never

13. 菲利普·锡德尼爵士

① stifling ['staiflɪŋ] a. 令人窒息的

② brook [bruk] n. 小溪

③ wistful ['wistful] a. 渴望的

残酷的激战之后，地面上到处是阵亡士兵的遗体和奄奄一息的伤员。空气又闷又热，太阳无情地照在那些躺在血泊里和尘土中的伤兵们身上。

伤员里面有一个贵族，此人温顺仁慈，深得大家的爱戴。可是现在是在战场上，比起最穷困的人，他也好不到哪儿。他也身负重伤，奄奄一息，遭受着伤痛和口渴难耐的双重折磨。

战争刚一结束，朋友们便赶过来救他。一个士兵手里捧着杯子向他跑来。

"来，菲利普爵士，"士兵说，"这是清凉的河水。我把您的头扶起来，您喝一口吧！"

杯子放到了菲利普爵士的嘴边，他满怀感激地望着这个士兵。忽然，菲利普爵士看见不远的地方躺着一个奄奄一息的士兵，此人脸上的表情再清楚不过了，他也口渴难耐。

"把水给他喝吧！"菲利普爵士立刻把杯子推向那个士兵，说："我的战友，你喝吧，你比我更需要它。"

菲利普爵士是一个多么勇敢而高尚的人啊！人们将

· 079 ·

be forgotten; for it was the name of a Christian gentleman who always had the good of others in his mind. Was it any wonder that everybody wept when it was heard that he was dead?

It is said, that, on the day when he was carried to the grave, every eye in the land was filled with tears. Rich and poor, high and low, all felt that they had lost a friend; all mourned the death of the kindest, gentlest man that they had ever known.

永远铭记这个基督教绅士的名字，他的心里永远装着别人。难怪当他牺牲的消息传来的时候，人们都难过地哭了起来。

据说在举行菲利普爵士葬礼的那一天，每个人的眼里都噙满了泪水。人们无论贫贱富贵，都感觉自己失去了一位朋友，都为这位最仁慈最绅士的朋友离世感到难过。

14. The Ungrateful Soldier

Here is another story of the battlefield, and it is much like the one which I have just told you.

Not quite a hundred years after the time of Sir Philip Sidney there was a war between the Swedes and the Danes. One day a great battle was fought, and the Swedes were beaten, and driven from the field. A soldier of the Danes who had been slightly wounded was sitting on the ground. He was about to take a drink from a **flask**[1]. All at once he heard some one say,—

"O sir! give me a drink, for I am dying."

It was a wounded Swede who spoke. He was lying on the ground only a little way off. The Dane went to him at once. He knelt down by the side of his fallen foe, and pressed the flask to his lips.

"Drink," said he, "for thy need is greater than mine."

Hardly had he spoken these words, when the Swede raised himself on his elbow. He pulled a pistol from his pocket, and shot at the man who would have befriended him. The bullet grazed the Dane's shoulder, but did not do him much harm.

"Ah, you **rascal**[2]!" he cried. "I was going to befriend you, and you repay me by trying to kill me. Now I will punish you. I would have given you all the water, but now you shall have only half." And with that he drank the half of it, and then gave the rest to the Swede.

14. 忘恩负义的士兵

这个故事依然发生在战场上，跟我刚才讲的那个相似。

菲利普·锡德尼爵士去世后不到一百年，瑞典人和丹麦人之间爆发了一场战争。一天，一场激战中瑞典人吃了败仗，被赶出了战场。一名受了轻伤的丹麦士兵坐在地上拿起水瓶准备喝水，忽然听到旁边有人说话：

"噢，先生！能不能给我喝一点，我快要不行了。"

原来是一个负了伤的瑞典兵，就躺在离丹麦兵不远的地方。丹麦兵立刻走过去跪下身子，把水瓶放到瑞典兵的嘴边。

"喝吧！"丹麦兵说，"你比我更需要喝水。"

可是还没等他把话说完，那个瑞典兵就用胳膊撑起身体，从口袋里拔出一只手枪，突然朝这个向他表示友好的人开了枪。子弹擦着丹麦兵的肩膀飞了出去，所幸并没有造成严重的伤害。

"啊，你这个混蛋！"丹麦兵大叫了起来，"我想帮助你，你却要我的命。现在我要惩罚你，本来我想把这些水都给你喝，现在只给你一半。"说完，他喝掉了一半的水，把剩下的另一半给了那个瑞典兵。

① flask [flɑ:sk] n. 长颈瓶

② rascal ['rɑ:skəl] n. 恶棍

When the King of the Danes heard about this, he sent for the soldier and had him tell the story just as it was.

"Why did you spare the life of the Swede after he had tried to kill you?" asked the king.

"Because, sir," said the soldier, "I could never kill a wounded enemy."

"Then you deserve to be a nobleman," said the king. And he rewarded him by making him a knight, and giving him a noble title.

丹麦国王听说了这件事，便派人把这个士兵叫来，让他把事情的经过再讲一遍。

"那个瑞典人要杀你，你为什么还要饶他的性命？"国王问。

"陛下，"士兵说，"我绝不会伤害一个受了伤的敌人。"

"你的品德高尚，理应成为一名贵族。"国王说。于是，国王册封这个士兵为骑士，还赐予他高贵的头衔。

15. Sir Humphrey Gilbert

More than three hundred years ago there lived in England a brave man whose name was Sir Humphrey Gilbert. At that time there were no white people in this country of ours. The land was covered with forests; and where there are now great cities and fine farms there were only trees and **swamps**[①] among which **roamed**[②] wild Indians and wild beasts.

Sir Humphrey Gilbert was one of the first men who tried to make a settlement in America. Twice did he bring men and ships over the sea, and twice did he fail, and sail back for England. The second time, he was on a little ship called the "Squirrel." Another ship, called the "Golden **Hind**[③]," was not far away. When they were three days from land, the wind failed, and the ships lay floating on the waves. Then at night the air grew very cold. A breeze sprang up from the east. Great white ice-bergs came drifting around them. In the morning the little ships were almost lost among the floating mountains of ice. The men on the "Hind" saw Sir Humphrey sitting on the **deck**[④] of the "Squirrel" with an open book in his hand. He called to them and said, —

"Be brave, my friends! We are as near heaven on the sea as on the land."

Night came again. It was a stormy night, with mist and rain. All at once the men on the "Hind" saw the lights on board of the "Squirrel" go out. The little **vessel**[⑤], with brave Sir Humphrey and all his brave men, was swallowed up by the waves.

15. 汉弗莱·吉尔伯特爵士

① swamp [swɔmp] n. 沼泽
② roam [rəum] v. 漫游

③ hind [haind] n. 雌马鹿

④ deck [dek] n. 甲板

⑤ vessel ['vesəl] n. 船

　　三百多年前，英格兰有一个勇敢的人名叫汉弗莱·吉尔伯特爵士。那时的美洲还没有白人，遍地是森林，现在的大城市和漂亮的农庄在当时还是一些树林和沼泽，还有野蛮的印第安人和野兽出没其中。

　　汉弗莱·吉尔伯特爵士是开拓美洲大陆的第一批人，曾两次带人远渡重洋，但最后都无功而返。在第二次航行中，汉弗莱·吉尔伯特爵士乘坐的小船名叫"松鼠"号，不远处是另外一艘小船"金鹿"号。离开陆地后的第三天，海上的风力变得很弱，小船只能随着波浪四处漂泊。到了夜里，天气开始变得寒冷起来，东边吹起了微风，巨大的白色冰山漂浮在小船的四周。第二天清晨，小船被冰山包围了起来，几乎不见了踪影。就在这时，"金鹿"号上的人看见汉弗莱·吉尔伯特爵士手捧着一本书，端坐在"松鼠"号的甲板上。汉弗莱·吉尔伯特爵士还朝他们大喊道："勇敢一点，我的朋友们！我们现在快接近天堂了，就跟我们在陆地上一样。"

　　夜幕再次降临，伴随着浓雾和暴雨，海上刮起了狂风。突然，"金鹿"号上的人发现"松鼠"号船上的灯熄灭了，原来海浪吞没了汉弗莱·吉尔伯特爵士和他的勇士们乘坐的那艘小船。

· 087 ·

16. Sir Walter Raleigh

There once lived in England a brave and noble man whose name was Walter Raleigh. He was not only brave and noble, but he was also handsome and polite; and for that reason the queen made him a knight, and called him Sir Walter Raleigh.

I will tell you about it.

When Raleigh was a young man, he was one day walking along a street in London. At that time the streets were not paved, and there were no sidewalks. Raleigh was dressed in very fine style, and he wore a beautiful scarlet **cloak**[①] thrown over his shoulders.

As he passed along, he found it hard work to keep from stepping in the mud, and soiling his handsome new shoes. Soon he came to a **puddle**[②] of muddy water which reached from one side of the street to the other. He could not step across. Perhaps he could jump over it.

As he was thinking what he should do, he happened to look up. Who was it coming down the street, on the other side of the puddle?

It was Elizabeth, the Queen of England, with her train of gentlewomen and waiting maids. She saw the dirty puddle in the street. She saw the handsome young man with the scarlet cloak, standing by the side of it. How was she to get across?

16. 沃尔特·雷利爵士

从前，英格兰有一个名叫沃尔特·雷利的人。此人不仅勇敢高贵、相貌堂堂，而且待人彬彬有礼，为此女王封他为骑士，称他沃尔特·雷利爵士。

下面，我就来讲一讲这个故事。

当时，雷利还是个年轻人。有一天，他穿着一套时尚的衣服走在伦敦街头，肩上披着漂亮的红色披风。当时的街道既没有铺路，也没有人行道。

雷利走着走着，发现前面的道路十分泥泞，脚上穿的漂亮新鞋子很难不被泥水弄脏。没过多久，雷利来到一个泥潭的前面。泥潭横跨整条街道，他迈不过去，要想过去就只能从泥潭上面跳过去。

正当雷利左右为难之际，忽然看见街道那头有人正往泥潭的另一边走来。

此人正是英格兰女王伊丽莎白，领着一队宫娥和侍女。女王看到街道上污浊的泥潭，又看见一个穿着红色披风的英俊青年站在另一边。女王寻思着，该怎么从这里走过去呢？

① cloak [kləuk] *n.* 披风

② puddle ['pʌdl] *n.* 泥潭

Fifty Famous Stories Retold

Young Raleigh, when he saw who was coming, forgot about himself. He thought only of helping the queen. There was only one thing that he could do, and no other man would have thought of that.

He took off his scarlet cloak, and spread it across the puddle. The queen could step on it now, as on a beautiful carpet.

She walked across. She was safely over the ugly puddle, and her feet had not touched the mud. She paused a moment, and thanked the young man.

As she walked **onward**[①] with her train, she asked one of the gentlewomen, "Who is that brave gentleman who helped us so handsomely?"

"His name is Walter Raleigh," said the gentle-woman.

"He shall have his reward," said the queen.

Not long after that, she sent for Raleigh to come to her palace.

The young man went, but he had no scarlet cloak to wear. Then, while all the great men and fine ladies of England stood around, the queen made him a knight. And from that time he was known as Sir Walter Raleigh, the queen's favorite.

Sir Walter Raleigh and Sir Humphrey Gilbert about whom I have already told you, were half-brothers.

When Sir Humphrey made his first voyage to America, Sir Walter was with him. After that, Sir Walter tried several times to send men to this country to make a settlement.

But those whom he sent found only great forests, and wild beasts, and **savage**[②] Indians. Some of them went back to England; some of them died **for want of**[③] food; and some of them were lost in the woods. At last Sir Walter gave up trying to get people to come to America.

But he found two things in this country which the people of England knew very little about. One was the potato, the other was tobacco.

If you should ever go to Ireland, you may be shown the place where Sir Walter planted the few potatoes which he carried over from America. He told his friends how the Indians used them for food; and he proved that they would grow in the Old World as well as in the New.

① onward ['ɔnwəd] ad. 向前

② savage ['sævidʒ] a. 野蛮的
③ for want of 因缺少……

年轻的雷利看到女王后便忘记了自己的处境，一心只想帮助女王。他知道现在只有一个办法，一个别人想不到的办法。

雷利把红披风从身上取下来铺在泥潭上，如此一来女王踩在上面，就像走在漂亮的红地毯上一样。

女王顺利通过了泥潭，脚上没有沾一丝污泥。她踌躇了一下，才向这个年轻人道谢。

女王领着队伍继续向前走，她问一个宫娥："那个如此慷慨帮助我们的勇敢绅士是谁？"

"是沃尔特·雷利。"宫娥回答说。

"他理应得到奖赏。"女王说。

不久之后，女王派人把雷利叫到王宫里。

年轻人去了，不过这次已经没有红色披风穿了。女王在英格兰所有达官贵妇的见证下，册封雷利为骑士。从那以后，人们都知道沃尔特·雷利爵士是女王的宠臣。

沃尔特·雷利爵士和前面提到过的汉弗莱·吉尔伯特爵士是同母异父的兄弟。

汉弗莱爵士第一次乘船去美洲时，同行的就有沃尔特爵士。之后，沃尔特爵士又几次派人前往新大陆试图定居。

但沃尔特爵士派出去的人发现，新大陆只有大片森林、野兽和野蛮的印第安人。这些人中有些返回了英格兰，有些因为食物短缺而被饿死，还有人在森林里迷了路，最终下落不明。迫不得已，沃尔特爵士只好放弃了差人去美洲的探险。

可是沃尔特爵士在新大陆上发现了马铃薯和烟草，在此之前英国人对这两样东西知之甚少。

如果你到访爱尔兰，或许会被带去参观一个沃尔特爵士种了少量马铃薯的地方，那是爵士从美洲带回来的。沃尔特爵士给朋友们讲述了印第安人食用马铃薯的

Sir Walter had seen the Indians smoking the leaves of the tobacco plant. He thought that he would do the same, and he carried some of the leaves to England. Englishmen had never used tobacco before that time; and all who saw Sir Walter **puffing**① away at a roll of leaves thought that it was a strange sight.

One day as he was sitting in his chair and smoking, his servant came into the room. The man saw the smoke **curling**② over his master's head, and he thought that he was on fire.

He ran out for some water. He found a **pail**③ that was quite full. He hurried back, and threw the water into Sir Walter's face. Of course the fire was all put out.

After that a great many men learned to smoke. And now tobacco is used in all countries of the world. It would have been well if Sir Walter Raleigh had let it alone.

① puff [pʌf] *v.* 吸，抽（香烟、烟斗等）

② curl [kə:l] *v.* 盘绕

③ pail [peil] *n.* 提桶

方法，而且证明马铃薯在英国同样可以像在美洲一样长得很好。

看到印第安人吸食烟叶，沃尔特爵士也想效仿，回去的时候就带了一些烟叶。在此之前英格兰从来没有人吸过烟草，人们看到沃尔特爵士吸着烟卷，嘴里喷着烟雾，都觉得十分奇怪。

一天，沃尔特爵士正坐在房间的椅子上吸烟，刚好仆人走了进来，看到主人的头顶上冒着烟，还以为他身上着火了。

仆人立刻跑到外面去找水。发现一只装满水的水桶后，便飞快地提回来泼到沃尔特爵士的脸上。当然，火被彻底浇灭了。

从那以后，很多人便开始学习抽烟，如今烟草已经传遍了全世界。假设当初瓦尔特爵士不去关注烟草那该多好啊！

17. Pocahontas

There was once a very brave man whose name was John Smith. He came to this country many years ago, when there were great woods everywhere, and many wild beasts and Indians. Many tales are told of his adventures, some of them true and some of them untrue. The most famous of all these is the following: —

One day when Smith was in the woods, some Indians came upon him, and made him their prisoner. They led him to their king, and in a short time they made ready to put him to death.

A large stone was brought in, and Smith was made to lie down with his head on it. Then two tall Indians with big **clubs**[1] in their hands came forward. The king and all his great men stood around to see. The Indians raised their clubs. In another moment they would fall on Smith's head.

But just then a little Indian girl rushed in. She was the daughter of the king, and her name was Pocahontas. She ran and threw herself between Smith and the uplifted clubs. She **clasped**[2] Smith's head with her arms. She laid her own head upon his.

"O father!" she cried, "**spare**[3] this man's life. I am sure he has done you no harm, and we ought to be his friends."

The men with the clubs could not strike, for they did not want to hurt the child. The king at first did not know what to do. Then he spoke to some of his

17. 波卡洪塔斯

从前，有一位勇士名叫约翰·史密斯。很多年前史密斯来到美洲的时候，这里不仅森林密布，而且还有很多野兽和印第安人。有关约翰·史密斯的冒险传说有许许多多，这些故事有些是真的，有些是假的，其中最有名的要数下面这个故事。

一天，史密斯在林中突然遭遇了印第安人的袭击，他们抓着他去见酋长，并且要马上将他处死。

印第安人搬来一块大石头，让史密斯躺下去把头放在上面。然后两个高个子的印第安人手拿大棒站在那里，酋长和头目们都在那里围观。两个印第安人举起手里的大棒，眼看就要落到史密斯的头上。

突然，一个印第安小姑娘冲了进来，原来是酋长的女儿，名叫波卡洪塔斯。她跑过来挡在史密斯和大棒之间，用手抱住史密斯的头，然后把自己的头放在他的头上面。

"啊，父亲！"小姑娘叫道，"饶了这个人吧！我相信他没有害过你，我们应该成为他的朋友。"

那两个印第安人不想伤及小女孩，于是手中的棍子便没有继续往下落。刚开始酋长也不知道如何是好，后

① club [klʌb] n. 棍棒

② clasp [klɑːsp] v. 抱紧

③ spare [spɛə] v. 饶恕

warriors[1], and they lifted Smith from the ground. They untied the **cords**[2] from his wrists and feet, and set him free.

The next day the king sent Smith home; and several Indians went with him to protect him from harm.

After that, as long as she lived, Pocahontas was the friend of the white men, and she did a great many things to help them.

① warrior ['wɔriə] n. 勇士
② cord [kɔːd] n. 绳索

来他对勇士们说了几句，让人把史密斯从地上抬起来，解开绑在他手脚上的绳子，然后把他放了。

第二天酋长送史密斯回家，还派了几个印第安人在身边保护他。

从此以后，只要波卡洪塔斯活着，就一直是白人的朋友。她做了很多有益于白人的事情。

18. George Washington and His Hatchet

When George Washington was quite a little boy, his father gave him a **hatchet**①. It was bright and new, and George took great delight in going about and chopping things with it.

He ran into the garden, and there he saw a tree which seemed to say to him, "Come and cut me down!"

18. 乔治·华盛顿和他的小斧头

① hatchet ['hætʃit] n. 短柄小斧

乔治·华盛顿年幼的时候，父亲送给他一把小斧头。这是一把崭新的斧头，乔治拿着它东砍西砍，玩得十分开心。

乔治跑到花园里面，看到那里有棵树好像在对他招着手说："快来，快来把我砍倒！"

George had often seen his father's men chop down the great trees in the forest, and he thought that it would be fine sport to see this tree fall with a crash to the ground. So he set to work with his little hatchet, and, as the tree was a very small one, it did not take long to lay it low.

Soon after that, his father came home.

"Who has been cutting my fine young cherry tree?" he cried. "It was the only tree of its kind in this country, and it cost me a great deal of money."

He was very angry when he came into the house.

"If I only knew who killed that cherry tree," he cried, "I would — yes, I would"—

"Father!" cried little George. "I will tell you the truth about it. I chopped the tree down with my hatchet."

His father forgot his anger.

"George," he said, and he took the little fellow in his arms, "George, I am glad that you told me about it. I would rather lose a dozen cherry trees than that you should tell one falsehood."

乔治过去经常看到父亲的佣人在森林里砍伐大树，心想要是这棵树一下子倒下来，那该是多么有趣的事情！于是他拿起小斧头开始砍树，树并不大，不一会儿工夫就被砍倒了。

没过多久父亲回来了。

"是谁砍倒了我那棵漂亮的小樱桃树？"父亲叫道，"这种树村子里面仅有一棵，是我花了大价钱才买回来的。"

说完，他怒气冲冲地走进家门。

"如果让我知道了是谁砍死了樱桃树，"他喊道，"我一定要……是的，我一定要……"

"爸爸！"小乔治吓得哭着说，"实话告诉你，这棵樱桃树是我用小斧头砍倒的。"

听到乔治的话，父亲竟然立刻忘记了愤怒。

"乔治，"他一边说，一边把小家伙抱了起来。"你没有撒谎，我很欣慰。我宁愿失去一打樱桃树，也不愿意听你撒一次谎。"

19. Grace Darling

It was a dark September morning. There was a storm at sea. A ship had been driven on a low rock off the shores of the Farne Islands. It had been broken in two by the waves, and half of it had been washed away. The other half lay yet on the rock, and those of the **crew**[1] who were still alive were clinging to it. But the waves were dashing over it, and in a little while it too would be carried to the bottom.

Could any one save the poor, half-drowned men who were there?

On one of the islands was a light-house; and there, all through that stormy night, Grace Darling had listened to the storm.

Grace was the daughter of the light-house keeper, and she had lived by the sea as long as she could remember.

In the darkness of the night, above the noise of the winds and waves, she heard screams and wild cries. When daylight came, she could see the **wreck**[2], a mile away, with the angry waters all around it. She could see the men clinging to the **masts**[3].

"We must try to save them!" she cried. "Let us go out in the boat at once!"

"It is of no use, Grace," said her father. "We cannot reach them."

19. 格蕾丝·达琳

　　九月的一个清晨，天空阴沉着，海上刮起了风暴，一艘船行驶至法恩群岛的海岸附近触礁了。船身被海浪撕成了两半，一半被海水冲走了，另一半搁浅在礁石上面。船上的幸存者死死地抓住剩下的半截船身，可是海浪依然不停地冲击着，也许要不了多长时间，这半截船身也要沉入海底。

　　有没有人去救那些快要被淹死的可怜人啊？

　　法恩群岛的一个岛上有一座灯塔。在整夜的狂风骤雨中，格蕾丝·达琳一直倾听着暴风雨的怒吼声。

　　格蕾丝是看守灯塔的人的女儿，自打记事起，就一直生活在海边。

　　在那个漆黑的夜里，格蕾丝听到了比狂风和海浪还要刺耳的尖叫和嘶喊声。天亮时分，她看到一英里远的地方有一只失事的船只，正被怒吼的海浪包围着。她还看到船上有人紧紧地抱着船的桅杆。

　　"我们一定要想办法救他们。"格蕾丝叫了起来，"我们马上划船过去！"

　　"格蕾丝，没用的，"她父亲说，"我们根本靠近不了他们。"

① crew [kru:] *n.* 全体船员

② wreck [rek] *n.* 残骸

③ mast [mɑ:st] *n.* 桅杆

· 103 ·

Fifty Famous Stories Retold

He was an old man, and he knew the force of the **mighty**① waves.

"We cannot stay here and see them die," said Grace. "We must at least try to save them."

Her father could not say, "No."

In a few minutes they were ready. They set off in the heavy lighthouse boat. Grace pulled one **oar**②, and her father the other, and they made straight toward the wreck. But it was hard rowing against such a sea, and it seemed as though they would never reach the place.

At last they were close to the rock, and now they were in greater danger than before. The fierce waves broke against the boat, and it would have been dashed in pieces, had it not been for the strength and skill of the brave girl.

But after many trials, Grace's father climbed upon the wreck, while Grace herself held the boat. Then one by one the worn-out crew were helped on board. It was all that the girl could do to keep the frail boat from being drifted away, or broken upon the sharp edges of the rock.

Then her father **clambered**③ back into his place. Strong hands grasped the oars, and by and by all were safe in the lighthouse. There Grace proved to be no less tender as a nurse than she had been brave as a sailor. She cared most kindly for the ship-wrecked men until the storm had died away and they were strong enough to go to their own homes.

All this happened a long time ago, but the name of Grace Darling will never be forgotten. She lies buried now in a little churchyard by the sea, not far from her old home. Every year many people go there to see her grave; and there a monument has been placed in honor of the brave girl. It is not a large monument, but it is one that speaks of the noble deed which made Grace Darling famous. It is a figure **carved**④ in stone of a woman lying at rest, with a boat's oar held fast in her right hand.

① mighty ['maiti] *a.* 强大的

② oar [ɔː] *n.* 桨

③ clamber ['klæmbə] *v.* (吃力地)爬上

④ carve [kɑːv] *v.* 雕刻

格蕾丝的父亲是一个老人,他知道海浪的威力有多大。

"可是我们不能待在这里眼睁睁看他们去死。"格蕾丝说,"不管怎么样,我们也应该试一试。"

父亲当然无法拒绝格蕾丝的请求。

几分钟之内,格蕾丝和父亲便做好了准备。他们乘着笨重的灯塔小船出发了,两人一人划着一支桨,朝着失事的船只径直划了过去。可是在那样的海浪中逆流而行实在太困难了,他们感到似乎永远也划不到那个地方。

最后两人终于靠近了那块礁石。可是他们现在却处于更大的危险之中,凶猛的海浪拍打着小船,如果不是格蕾丝的力气和技术,小船恐怕早就被海浪拍成了碎片。

经过一次次的努力之后,格蕾丝的父亲终于爬上了那片残骸。格蕾丝则拼尽全力努力支撑着小船,使它不被海浪冲走撞到尖锐的礁石上面,那些筋疲力尽的船员们一个个被救了上来。

最后格蕾丝的父亲爬回小船,用强有力的大手握住船桨使劲划着。不一会儿,所有人都平安地抵达了灯塔。这时格蕾丝又从一个勇敢的水手变成一个温柔的护士,细心照顾那些遭受了海难的人们,一直等到暴风雨过去,水手们的体力恢复到可以回家为止。

所有这一切都发生在很多年以前。从那以后,人们永远记住了格蕾丝·达琳的名字。如今,格蕾丝被安葬在海边小教堂的墓地里,那里离她的家乡不远。墓地里面还立了一块纪念碑,用来纪念这个勇敢无畏的女孩,每年都有许多人前来凭吊。尽管墓碑不大,却讲述着格蕾丝为人称道的高尚行为,上面刻着一个躺在那里休息的女人,右手紧紧握着一支船桨。

20. The Story of William Tell

The people of Switzerland were not always free and happy as they are today. Many years ago a proud **tyrant**①, whose name was Gessler, ruled over them, and made their **lot**② a bitter one indeed.

One day this tyrant set up a tall **pole**③ in the public square, and put his own cap on the top of it; and then he gave orders that every man who came into the town should bow down before it. But there was one man, named William Tell, who would not do this. He stood up straight with folded arms, and laughed at the swinging cap. He would not bow down to Gessler himself.

When Gessler heard of this, he was very angry. He was afraid that other men would disobey, and that soon the whole country would **rebel**④ against him. So he made up his mind to punish the **bold**⑤ man.

William Tell's home was among the mountains, and he was a famous hunter. No one in all the land could shoot with bow and arrow so well as he. Gessler knew this, and so he thought of a cruel plan to make the hunter's own skill bring him to grief. He ordered that Tell's little boy should be made to stand up in the public square with an apple on his head; and then he **bade**⑥ Tell shoot the apple with one of his arrows.

Tell begged the tyrant not to have him make this test of his skill. What if the boy should move? What if the bowman's hand should **tremble**⑦? What if the

20. 威廉·泰尔的故事

① tyrant ['tairənt] n. 暴君，恶霸
② lot [lɔt] n. 命运
③ pole [pəul] n. 杆

④ rebel [ri'bel] v. 反叛
⑤ bold [bəuld] a. 大胆的

⑥ bade [beid] v.（bid 的一种过去式）命令

⑦ tremble ['trembl] v. 发抖

从前，瑞士人生活得并不像今天这样快乐和自由。很多年前，那里有一个狂妄的恶霸统治官名叫盖斯勒，人民在他的统治下过着十分痛苦的生活。

一天，这个恶霸在广场上立起一根长竿，然后把自己的帽子顶在上面，下令凡是进城的人都必须在帽子前面弯腰行礼。然而，有一个名叫威廉·泰尔的人拒不服从，他抱紧双臂，笔直地站在那里，嘲笑着那顶摇摇晃晃的帽子。就是盖斯勒本人站在那里，他也不会弯腰鞠躬。

盖斯勒听说此事后大为震怒，害怕其他人也不服从。如果那样，整个国家的人都会起来反抗他。于是，他决心要惩罚这个胆大包天的家伙。

威廉·泰尔家住群山之中，是一个有名的猎人。他的箭术非常高明，举世无双。盖斯勒知道此事后，便想出了一条恶计，想让猎人用自己的箭术来惩罚自己。他命令泰尔的小儿子头顶一只苹果站在广场上，然后让泰尔用箭去射苹果。

泰尔恳求恶霸不要用这样的手段来考验他的箭术。试想，如果小孩身体移动了会怎么样？假如射手的手颤

arrow should not carry true?

"Will you make me kill my boy?" he said.

"Say no more," said Gessler. "You must hit the apple with your one arrow. If you fail, my soldiers shall kill the boy before your eyes."

Then, without another word, Tell fitted the arrow to his bow. He took aim, and let it fly. The boy stood firm and still. He was not afraid, for he had all faith in his father's skill.

The arrow whistled through the air. It struck the apple fairly in the center, and carried it away. The people who saw it shouted with joy.

As Tell was turning away from the place, an arrow which he had hidden under his coat dropped to the ground.

"Fellow!" cried Gessler, "what mean you with this second arrow?"

"Tyrant!" was Tell's proud answer, "this arrow was for your heart if I had hurt my child."

And there is an old story, that, not long after this, Tell did shoot the tyrant with one of his arrows; and thus he set his country free.

抖了会怎么样？假如箭射偏了又会怎么样？

"你这不是叫我亲手杀死自己的孩子吗？"泰尔说。

"住口！"盖斯勒说，"你要么一箭射中苹果，要么我就让士兵在你面前把孩子杀掉。"

泰尔没有再多说一句话。他把箭搭在弓上，瞄准目标，然后射了出去。那个男孩站在那里一动不动，心里并没有感到害怕。对于父亲的箭术，他有十足的把握。

那支箭"嗖"的一声划过天空，不偏不倚正中靶心，苹果被射飞出去。围观的人都欢呼了起来。

泰尔从原地转过身。忽然，他在外套里藏的另一支箭掉在了地上。

"你这个家伙！"盖斯勒大声叫道，"你想用那支箭干什么？"

"恶霸！"泰勒骄傲地回答说，"一旦我失手误伤了孩子，这支箭就会射向你的心脏。"

从那以后便开始流传一个古老的故事：传说在此后不久，泰尔真的用箭射死了恶霸，使他的国家重新获得了自由。

21. Arnold Winkelried

A great army was marching into Switzerland. If it should go much farther, there would be no driving it out again. The soldiers would burn the towns, they would rob the farmers of their grain and sheep, they would make slaves of the people.

The men of Switzerland knew all this. They knew that they must fight for their homes and their lives. And so they came from the mountains and valleys to try what they could do to save their land. Some came with bows and arrows, some with **scythes**[1] and **pitchforks**[2], and some with only sticks and clubs.

But their **foes**[3] kept in line as they marched along the road. Every soldier was fully armed. As they moved and kept close together, nothing could be seen of them but their **spears**[4] and **shields**[5] and shining **armor**[6]. What could the poor country people do against such foes as these?

"We must break their lines," cried their leader; "for we cannot harm them while they keep together."

The bowmen shot their arrows, but they **glanced off**[7] from the soldiers' shields. Others tried clubs and stones, but with no better luck. The lines were still unbroken. The soldiers moved steadily onward; their shields lapped over one another; their thousand spears looked like so many long **bristles**[8] in the sunlight. What cared they for sticks and stones and huntsmen's arrows?

"If we cannot break their ranks," said the Swiss, "we have no chance for

21. 阿诺德·温克里德

① scythe [scythe] *n.* 长柄大镰刀
② pitchfork ['pitʃfɔːk] *n.* 长柄草耙
③ foe [fəu] *n.* 敌人
④ spear [spiə] *n.* 矛
⑤ shield [ʃiːld] *n.* 盾
⑥ armor ['ɑːmə] *n.* 盔甲

⑦ glance off 擦过，掠过

⑧ bristle ['brisl] *n.* 刚毛

  敌人的一支大部队正在向瑞士开来，如果任其继续前进，就再也无法把他们赶出瑞士。接下来他们就会烧杀抢掠，将民众变成他们的奴隶。
  瑞士人对此十分清楚，知道必须为自己的家园和生命力战到底。他们纷纷走出山岭谷地聚在一起，商议怎样才能拯救自己的国家。这些人来的时候携带着弓箭、镰刀和草耙，还有些人只带了棍棒。
  然而他们面对的敌人却全副武装，行军的队伍阵型整齐。他们集结成密集队形行进时，除了能够看见长矛、盾牌和闪闪发光的盔甲，就什么也看不到了。这些可怜的乡下人又怎么是这些强敌的对手呢？
  "我们必须冲破敌人的队形。"领头的瑞士人喊道，"如果让他们围在一起，我们就没有办法伤到他们。"
  弓箭手的箭射在敌人的盾牌上纷纷弹开，用棍棒和石头攻击他们也无济于事。敌军的队形没有乱，仍然在继续前进，他们的盾牌相互交叠，数千支长矛就像许许多多长刺，在阳光下闪闪发光。他们怎么会害怕瑞士人的棍棒、石头和射出的箭呢？
  "如果冲不破敌人的队形，"那个瑞士人说，"就没

· 111 ·

fight, and our country will be lost!"

Then a poor man, whose name was Arnold Winkelried, stepped out.

"On the side of **yonder**[①] mountain," said he, "I have a happy home. There my wife and children wait for my return. But they will not see me again, for this day I will give my life for my country. And do you, my friends, do your duty, and Switzerland shall be free."

With these words he ran forward. "Follow me!" he cried to his friends. "I will break the lines, and then let every man fight as bravely as he can."

He had nothing in his hands, neither club nor stone nor other weapon. But he ran straight onward to the place where the spears were thickest.

"Make way for **liberty**[②]!" he cried, as he dashed right into the lines.

A hundred spears were turned to catch him upon their points. The soldiers forgot to stay in their places. The lines were broken. Arnold's friends rushed bravely after him. They fought with whatever they had in hand. They **snatched**[③] spears and shields from their foes. They had no thought of fear. They only thought of their homes and their dear native land. And they won at last.

Such a battle no one ever knew before. But Switzerland was saved, and Arnold Winkelried did not die **in vain**[④].

① yonder [ˈjɔndə] a. 远处的

② liberty [ˈlibəti] n. 自由

③ snatch [snætʃ] v. 抢夺

④ in vain 无效

有办法打击他们，我们就要亡国！"

这时，一个叫阿诺德·温克里德的穷人站了出来。

"翻过高山，"他说，"是我幸福的家，妻子和孩子正在家中等着我回去。可是他们再也见不到我了，因为就在今天，我要把自己的生命献给祖国。而你们，我的朋友们，也要担负起自己的责任，只有那样，瑞士才能获得自由。"

说完，阿诺德·温克里德带头冲了出去。"跟我来！"他向朋友们喊道，"我要冲破敌人的队形，我们每个人都要奋勇作战。"

当时阿诺德·温克里德真的是手无寸铁，没有棍棒石头，也没有其他武器，径直向长矛最密集的地方冲去。

"为了自由，冲啊！"阿诺德·温克里德一边喊着，一边冲向敌人的队伍。

敌军的上百支长矛一起向阿诺德·温克里德刺来，士兵们忘记了自己的位置，阵形开始大乱。阿诺德的朋友们紧跟着他勇敢地冲了过去，用手中的家伙与敌人搏斗。他们抢夺敌人的长矛和盾牌，丝毫不感到害怕，心里只想着自己的家园和亲爱的祖国。最后，他们终于取得了胜利。

这是一场空前绝后的战斗。瑞士得救了，阿诺德·温克里德的鲜血没有白流。

22. The Bell of Atri

Atri is the name of a little town in Italy. It is a very old town, and is built halfway up the side of a steep hill.

A long time ago, the King of Atri bought a fine large bell, and had it hung up in a tower in the market place. A long rope that reached almost to the ground was fastened to the bell. The smallest child could ring the bell by pulling upon this rope.

"It is the bell of justice," said the king.

When at last everything was ready, the people of Atri had a great holiday. All the men and women and children came down to the market place to look at the bell of justice. It was a very pretty bell, and was polished until it looked almost as bright and yellow as the sun.

"How we should like to hear it ring!" they said.

Then the king came down the street.

"Perhaps he will ring it," said the people; and everybody stood very **still**①, and waited to see what he would do.

But he did not ring the bell. He did not even take the rope in his hands. When he came to the foot of the tower, he stopped, and raised his hand.

"My people," he said, "do you see this beautiful bell? It is your bell; but it must never be rung except in case of need. If any one of you is **wronged**② at any

22. 阿特里的钟

阿特里是意大利一座古老的小城，位于一个陡峭的半山腰上。

很久以前，阿特里国王买来一座精美的大钟，让人挂在市场内的塔楼上。这个大钟上捆着一根绳子，绳子几乎垂到地面上，即便年龄最小的孩子也能拉着它敲钟。

"这是一座正义之钟。"国王说。

一切准备就绪之后，阿特里的民众举行了一场盛大的节日庆典，男女老少都涌到市场上观看这座正义之钟。那是一座多么漂亮的钟啊，被擦拭得像太阳一样金光灿灿。

"我们好想听到钟声！"他们说。

就在这时候，国王走上了街头。

"可能国王要摇响大钟。"人们都在议论着，静静站在那里等待国王的下一个动作。

可是国王并没有摇响大钟，他的手甚至连钟绳也没有碰一下。他走到塔楼下面，举起了手。

"我的子民们，"国王说，"你们都看见这座漂亮的大钟了吧？它是你们的钟，只有需要的时候才可以敲响

① still [stil] *a.* 静止的

② wrong [rɔŋ] *v.* 不公正地对待

· 115 ·

time, he may come and ring the bell; and then the judges shall come together at once, and hear his case, and give him justice. Rich and poor, old and young, all alike may come; but no one must touch the rope unless he knows that he has been wronged."

Many years passed by after this. Many times did the bell in the market place ring out to call the judges together. Many wrongs were righted, many ill-doers were punished. At last the **hempen**[1] rope was almost worn out. The lower part of it was untwisted; some of the strands were broken; it became so short that only a tall man could reach it.

"This will never do," said the judges one day. "What if a child should be wronged? It could not ring the bell to let us know it."

They gave orders that a new rope should be put upon the bell at once,—a rope that should hang down to the ground, so that the smallest child could reach it. But there was not a rope to be found in all Atri. They would have to send across the mountains for one, and it would be many days before it could be brought. What if some great wrong should be done before it came? How could the judges know about it, if the injured one could not reach the old rope?

"Let me fix it for you," said a man who stood by.

He ran into his garden, which was not far away, and soon came back with a long grapevine in his hands.

"This will do for a rope," he said; and he climbed up, and **fastened**[2] it to the bell. The **slender**[3] vine, with its leaves and **tendrils**[4] still upon it, **trailed**[5] to the ground.

"Yes," said the judges, "it is a very good rope. Let it be as it is."

Now, on the hillside above the village, there lived a man who had once been a brave knight. In his youth he had ridden through many lands, and he had fought in many a battle. His best friend through all that time had been his horse, — a strong, noble **steed**[6] that had borne him safe through many a danger.

① hempen ['hempən] *a.* 大麻制的

② fasten ['fɑːsən] *v.* 扎牢
③ slender ['slendə] *a.* 细长的
④ tendril ['tendril] *n.* 卷须
⑤ trail [treil] *v.* 下垂

⑥ steed [stiːd] *n.* 战马

它。不管什么时候，只要有谁蒙受了冤屈，就可以敲响它，法官就会立刻赶来审他的案子，为他主持公道。不管什么人，无论贫富老少，人人都一样，但条件是他们必须觉得自己遭受了委屈，否则谁人也不允许碰那根绳子。"

许多年过去了，市场上的钟响了一次又一次，法官们一次次赶过来审判案子，很多冤案都得到了昭雪，坏人得到了惩罚。后来，钟上面的那根绳子磨损得差不多了，下端开始散开，有几股绳子已经断掉，绳子的长度也短到只有个高的人才能够到。

"这样可不行。"有一天法官们说，"如果小孩子受了委屈该怎么办？他就不能敲钟让我们知道了。"

于是，法官们决定马上给大钟换一根新绳，绳子的长度要能够垂到地面上，这样一来，即使年龄再小的孩子也能够拉到。可是他们把全阿特里城找遍了，也找不出那样的一根绳子，于是只好派人翻山到别处去买。而要买到绳子需要好几天的时间，万一在此期间出现大的冤屈该怎么办？如果受害人够不到那根旧绳子，法官又怎样能够知道他的冤屈呢？

"我来把它修好。"一个站在旁边的人说。

此人跑到不远处自己家的花园里，很快便拿着一根长长的葡萄藤回来了。

"可以用这个来代替绳子。"他说完就爬上去把葡萄藤系在钟上面，这条带着叶子和卷须的细藤一直垂到了地面上。

"太好了！"法官们说，"真是一根好绳子，就这样办吧！"

当时，村子高处的山坡上住着一个勇敢的骑士。这个骑士年轻的时候曾经骑马去过许多地方，也参加过很多次战斗。在那些日子里，他的马是陪伴他最好的朋友。那是一匹健壮而高贵的战马，曾经载着他平安闯过了许多危险。

Fifty Famous Stories Retold

But the knight, when he grew older, cared no more to ride into battle; he cared no more to do brave deeds; he thought of nothing but gold; he became a **miser**①. At last he sold all that he had, except his horse, and went to live in a little hut on the hillside. Day after day he sat among his money bags, and planned how he might get more gold; and day after day his horse stood in his bare **stall**②, half-starved, and shivering with cold.

"What is the use of keeping that lazy steed?" said the miser to himself one morning. "Every week it costs me more to keep him than he is worth. I might sell him; but there is not a man that wants him. I cannot even give him away. I will turn him out to shift for himself, and pick grass by the roadside. If he starves to death, so much the better."

So the brave old horse was turned out to find what he could among the rocks on the **barren**③ hillside. **Lame**④ and sick, he strolled along the dusty roads, glad to find a blade of grass or a **thistle**⑤. The boys threw stones at him, the dogs barked at him, and in all the world there was no one to pity him.

One hot afternoon, when no one was upon the street, the horse chanced to wander into the market place. Not a man nor child was there, for the heat of the sun had driven them all indoors. The gates were wide open; the poor beast could roam where he pleased. He saw the grapevine rope that hung from the bell of justice. The leaves and tendrils upon it were still fresh and green, for it had not been there long. What a fine dinner they would be for a starving horse!

He stretched his thin neck, and took one of the tempting **morsels**⑥ in his mouth. It was hard to break it from the vine. He pulled at it, and the great bell above him began to ring. All the people in Atri heard it. It seemed to say, —

"Some one   has done   me wrong!

① miser ['maizə] n. 守财奴

② stall [stɔ:l] n. 马厩

③ barren ['bærən] a. 贫瘠的
④ lame [leim] a. 跛足的
⑤ thistle ['θisl] n. [植] 蓟

⑥ morsel ['mɔ:sel] n.（少量）佳肴

可是骑士上了年纪后，就再也不想骑马打仗了，也不想去建什么英勇的功绩，他心里只有金子，变成了一个守财奴。最后他变卖了所有家当，只留下那匹马，并且把家搬到山腰上的一间小屋里。日复一日，他坐在自己的钱袋子中间，算计着怎样才能弄到更多的金子；而他的马却站在露天的马厩里，在寒风中冷得全身发抖，过着饥一顿饱一顿的日子。

"留着这匹懒马还有什么用？"一天早晨，这个守财奴自言自语道，"每个星期花那么多钱养它越来越不划算了。我想把它卖掉，又没有人要，想送人也送不出去。干脆把它赶走得了，让它自己吃路边的草自生自灭，如果饿死了，那就更好！"

于是，这匹勇敢的老马被赶到贫瘠的山坡上，只好在乱石中间找草吃。它瘸着腿，病怏怏地流浪在尘土飞扬的马路上，有时即便找到一根草一片蓟叶都会感到高兴。孩子们朝它扔石头，狗冲着它汪汪叫，世界上没有一个人怜悯它。

一个炎热的下午，街上空无一人，这匹老马来到市场上。当时那里没有大人，也没有小孩，火热的太阳把大家都赶到了屋内。城门大开着，这匹可怜的畜生想去哪儿就可以去哪儿。忽然，它看见挂在正义之钟上面的葡萄藤，由于挂的时间不长，上面的叶子和卷须依然新鲜碧绿。对于一匹饥饿的马来说，这将是多好的一顿美餐啊！

于是老马伸出瘦削的脖子，用嘴去啃那诱人的美餐。可是要把藤咬断不那么容易，老马用力地扯着，上面的大钟就跟着响了起来，钟声传到阿特里人的耳朵里，仿佛正在诉说：

"有人对我不公！

Fifty Famous Stories Retold

> *Some one has done me wrong!*
> *Oh! come and judge my case!*
> *Oh! come and judge my case!*
> *For I've been wronged!"*

The judges heard it. They put on their robes, and went out through the hot streets to the market place. They wondered who it could be who would ring the bell at such a time. When they passed through the gate, they saw the old horse **nibbling**① at the vine.

"Ha!" cried one, "it is the miser's steed. He has come to call for justice; for his master, as everybody knows, has treated him most **shamefully**②."

"He **pleads his cause**③ as well as any dumb brute can," said another.

"And he shall have justice!" said the third.

"Some one has done me wrong!"

Meanwhile a crowd of men and women and children had come into the market

· 120 ·

有人对我不公！

快！快来审我的案子吧！

快！快来审我的案子吧！

因为我受了委屈！"

　　法官们听见钟声立刻穿上了长袍，从大街上来到市场里面，他们想不出来会有谁在这个时间敲钟。他们穿过大门，看见一匹老马正在啃那根葡萄藤。

　　"哈！"有人叫道，"是那个守财奴的马，它是来寻求正义的，大家都知道它主人对它有多无情无义。"

　　"它虽是个不会说话的畜生，却也能为自己申冤。"另一个人说。

　　"它理应得到公道！"第三个人又说。

① nibble ['nibl] v. 一点一点地咬
② shamefully ['ʃeimfəli] ad. 不体面地
③ plead one's cause 为某人申冤

"有人对我不公！"

　　这时一群男女老少拥到广场上，想知道法官究竟要

place, eager to learn what cause the judges were about to try. When they saw the horse, all stood still in wonder. Then every one was ready to tell how they had seen him wandering on the hills, unfed, uncared for, while his master sat at home counting his bags of gold.

"Go bring the miser before us," said the judges.

And when he came, they bade him stand and hear their judgment.

"This horse has served you well for many a year," they said. "He has saved you from many a **peril**①. He has helped you gain your wealth. Therefore we order that one half of all your gold shall be set aside to buy him shelter and food, a green **pasture**② where he may graze, and a warm stall to comfort him in his old age."

The miser hung his head, and **grieved**③ to lose his gold; but the people shouted with joy, and the horse was led away to his new stall and a dinner such as he had not had in many a day.

审理什么案子。看到那匹老马后，他们都惊奇地呆站在那里。然后，每个人都等不及要说一说他们是怎样看见这匹老马在山坡上流浪的，它没有东西吃，也没有人照顾，而它的主人却坐在家里数着成袋成袋的金子。

"去把那个守财奴叫来。"法官们说。

那个守财奴来了以后，法官们命令他站在那儿听他们的审判。

"这匹马服侍了你这么多年，"法官们说，"在许多危机的关头，它曾经救过你的性命，也为你赢得了财富，所以你要拿出一半金子来为他解决栖身之处和食物，要有一片绿色的牧场供它吃草，一间温暖的马厩供它安度晚年。"

守财奴的头垂了下去，他为即将失去的金子而感到沮丧，而围观的人们则欢呼了起来。那匹老马被带到新的马厩里面，吃上了很多年都没有吃到过的美餐。

① peril ['peril] *n.* 危险

② pasture ['pɑːstʃə] *n.* 草地
③ grieve [griːv] *v.* 悲痛

23. How Napoleon Crossed the Alps

About a hundred years ago there lived a great general whose name was Napoleon Bonaparte. He was the leader of the French army; and France was at war with nearly all the countries around. He wanted very much to take his soldiers into Italy; but between France and Italy there are high mountains called the Alps, the tops of which are covered with snow.

"Is it possible to cross the Alps?" said Napoleon.

The men who had been sent to look at the **passes**[1] over the mountains shook their heads. Then one of them said, "It may be possible, but —"

"Let me hear no more," said Napoleon. "Forward to Italy!"

People laughed at the thought of an army of sixty thousand men crossing the Alps where there was no road. But Napoleon waited only to see that everything was in good order, and then he gave the order to march.

The long line of soldiers and horses and **cannon**[2] stretched for twenty miles. When they came to a steep place where there seemed to be no way to go farther, the **trumpets**[3] sounded "Charge!" Then every man did his best, and the whole army moved right onward.

Soon they were safe over the Alps. In four days they were marching on the plains of Italy.

23. 拿破仑翻越阿尔卑斯山

大约一百年前，有一个伟大的将军名叫拿破仑·波拿巴，是法国军队的最高统帅，当时法国跟几乎每一个邻国都在交战。拿破仑将军想带兵进入意大利，可是法国和意大利之间隔着一座名叫阿尔卑斯的大山，山顶上常年覆盖着皑皑积雪。

"我们有没有可能翻越阿尔卑斯山？"拿破仑问。

那些被派到各个山口探路的人都摇着头，只有一个人说："也许有可能，但是……"

"我不想再听你们多说什么！"拿破仑说，"向意大利挺进！"

六万人的军队想穿越无路可走的阿尔卑斯山，人们听到这个想法后都不禁笑了起来。一切准备妥当之后，拿破仑便下令开始行军。

由士兵、马匹和大炮组成的队伍一直绵延了二十英里。他们到达一个十分险峻的地方，发现几乎无路可走。就在那个时候，冲锋的号角响了起来，于是所有人都拼尽了全力，整个部队一往无前地向前挺进着。

很快，拿破仑的军队便翻过了阿尔卑斯山。四天之后，他们行军在意大利平原上。

---

① pass [pɑːs] *n.* 关口，要隘

② cannon ['kænən] *n.* 大炮
③ trumpet ['trʌmpit] *n.* 喇叭

"The man who has made up his mind to win," said Napoleon, "will never say 'Impossible.'"

"一个决心取得胜利的人,"拿破仑说,"嘴里是永远不会说'办不到'的。"

24. The Story of Cincinnatus

There was a man named Cincinnatus who lived on a little farm not far from the city of Rome. He had once been rich, and had held the highest office in the land; but in one way or another he had lost all his wealth. He was now so poor that he had to do all the work on his farm with his own hands. But in those days it was thought to be a noble thing to till the soil.

Cincinnatus was so wise and just that everybody trusted him, and asked his advice; and when any one was in trouble, and did not know what to do, his neighbors would say,—

"Go and tell Cincinnatus. He will help you."

Now there lived among the mountains, not far away, a tribe of fierce, half-wild men, who were at war with the Roman people. They persuaded another tribe of bold warriors to help them, and then marched toward the city, plundering and robbing as they came. They **boasted**[1] that they would **tear down**[2] the walls of Rome, and burn the houses, and kill all the men, and make slaves of the women and children.

At first the Romans, who were very proud and brave, did not think there was much danger. Every man in Rome was a soldier, and the army which went out to fight the robbers was the finest in the world. No one stayed at home with the women and children and boys but the white-haired "Fathers," as they were called,

24. 辛辛那图斯的故事

从前，有个名叫辛辛那图斯的人，住在距离罗马城不远的小农庄里。此人曾经十分富有，而且在当地身居高位，可是由于某些原因，他失去了所有的财富。现在辛辛那图斯在经济上十分拮据，农庄里的所有活都要靠自己来完成。不过在当时那个年代里，耕田种地还被认为是一件高尚的事情呢！

辛辛那图斯既聪明又公正，大家都信任他，愿意让他为自己的事情出谋划策。不管什么人遇到麻烦，邻居们就会说：

"去找辛辛那图斯，他会帮助你的。"

当时，群山里面有一个凶狠野蛮的部族正在和罗马人交战，在游说成功另一个勇猛好斗的部族之后，他们一起向罗马城进军。这些人一路上肆意掠夺抢劫，还扬言要拆毁罗马的城墙，烧掉房屋，把所有男人都杀死，将女人和小孩都变成奴隶。

骄傲勇敢的罗马人刚开始认为并不存在多大的危险。罗马城里的男人个个都是战士，出去与强盗战斗的部队也是世界上最优秀的。罗马城除了那些掌管罗马法律的白发元老们和守城的一小队人马外，城里只剩下妇

① boast [bəust] v. 夸口说
② tear down 拆毁

· 129 ·

who made the laws for the city, and a small company of men who guarded the walls. Everybody thought that it would be an easy thing to drive the men of the mountains back to the place where they belonged.

But one morning five horsemen came riding down the road from the mountains. They rode with great speed; and both men and horses were covered with dust and blood. The watchman at the gate knew them, and shouted to them as they **galloped**[①] in. Why did they ride thus? and what had happened to the Roman army?

They did not answer him, but rode into the city and along the quiet streets; and everybody ran after them, eager to find out what was the matter. Rome was not a large city at that time; and soon they reached the market place where the white-haired Fathers were sitting. Then they leaped from their horses, and told their story.

"Only yesterday," they said, "our army was marching through a narrow valley between two steep mountains. All at once a thousand savage men sprang out from among the rocks before us and above us. They had blocked up the way; and the pass was so narrow that we could not fight. We tried to come back; but they had blocked up the way on this side of us too. The fierce men of the mountains were before us and behind us, and they were throwing rocks down upon us from above. We had been caught in a trap. Then ten of us set **spurs**[②] to our horses; and five of us forced our way through, but the other five fell before the spears of the mountain men. And now, O Roman Fathers! Send help to our army at once, or every man will be **slain**[③], and our city will be taken."

"What shall we do?" said the white-haired Fathers. "Whom can we send but the guards and the boys? and who is wise enough to lead them, and thus save Rome?"

All shook their heads and were very grave; for it seemed as if there was no hope. Then one said, "Send for Cincinnatus. He will help us."

Cincinnatus was in the field **plowing**[④] when the men who had been sent to him came **in great haste**[⑤]. He stopped and greeted them kindly, and waited for

女和儿童,大家原以为要把那些山里来的家伙赶回老家,是一件不费吹灰之力的事情。

可是有一天早晨,五个骑兵从山里面飞奔而来,人和马的身上布满了尘土和鲜血。守城的士兵认识这几个人,看见他们飞奔过来,便朝他们大声喊:出什么事了,你们为什么跑得这么快?罗马军队出什么事情了?

那些骑兵根本无暇理会这个士兵,径直沿着寂静的街道奔进了城里。众人都一起跟在他们后面跑,想知道究竟出了什么事。那时的罗马城面积还不大,他们很快就来到集市上,白发元老们都坐在那里。骑兵跳下马,开始描述他们自己的亲身遭遇。

"就在昨天,"他们说,"我们的军队走到一个狭窄的山谷里面,两边都是陡峭的山峰。突然,一千个野蛮人从岩石堆里跳出来,堵住了我们的去路。那个通道非常窄,我们根本无法还击。等我们想折返回去,来路已经被敌人堵死。那些凶恶的山里人前后夹击,还从山上朝下面扔石头,我们的部队落入了敌人的包围圈。我们十个人想拼死冲出来报信,结果只有五个人杀出了重围,另外五个人都倒在敌人的长矛之下。罗马的元老们,现在要赶快派人去增援,否则我们就要全军覆灭,罗马城也将不保。"

"我们该怎么办?"白发元老们问,"现在除了守城的卫兵和男孩子,还能派谁去?谁有足够的智慧带领他们来挽救罗马城?"

所有人都摇着头,心情变得十分沉重,似乎感到已经没有希望了。忽然有一个人说:"请辛辛那图斯来,他能帮助我们。"

当时辛辛那图斯正在田里面耕地,看到有人急匆匆赶过来,就停下手中的活热情地跟他们打招呼,等着听

① gallop ['gæləp] v. 疾驰

② spur [spɜː] n. 马刺

③ slain [slein] v.(slay 的过去分词)杀死

④ plow [plau] n. 犁,耕地
⑤ in great haste 匆匆

· 131 ·

them to speak.

"Put on your cloak, Cincinnatus," they said, "and hear the words of the Roman people."

Then Cincinnatus wondered what they could mean. "Is all well with Rome?" he asked; and he called to his wife to bring him his cloak.

She brought the cloak; and Cincinnatus wiped the dust from his hands and arms, and threw it over his shoulders. Then the men told their **errand**①.

They told him how the army with all the noblest men of Rome had been entrapped in the mountain pass. They told him about the great danger the city was in. Then they said, "The people of Rome make you their ruler and the ruler of their city, to do with everything as you choose; and the Fathers bid you come at once and go out against our enemies, the fierce men of the mountains."

So Cincinnatus left his plow standing where it was, and hurried to the city. When he passed through the streets, and gave orders as to what should be done, some of the people were afraid, for they knew that he had all power in Rome to

他们讲明来意。

"快把外套穿上，辛辛那图斯。"来人说，"去听听罗马人正在议论什么。"

辛辛那图斯不明白对方的来意。"罗马城一切安好吧？"他问，然后叫妻子把外套拿给他。

外套拿来了，辛辛那图斯拭去身上的尘土，赶忙把衣服披上。紧接着，来人讲明了他们的来意。

他们给辛辛那图斯讲这支罗马贵族组成的军队如何被困在山隘里，罗马城现在正处于空前的危险之中。接着他们又说："现在，罗马人要把自己和罗马城交给你来统帅，你可以按照自己的意愿去行事。元老们命你立刻随我们来，赶去迎击敌军，那是一些十分凶悍的山里人。"

① errand ['erənd] *n.* 差使

辛辛那图斯把犁丢在地里，立刻赶往罗马城。他穿过大街小巷，一路发号施令，大家都对他心存敬畏，因为他们知道，辛辛那图斯现在掌握着罗马的最高权力。

· 133 ·

Fifty Famous Stories Retold

do what he pleased. But he armed the guards and the boys, and went out at their head to fight the fierce mountain men, and free the Roman army from the trap into which it had fallen.

A few days afterward there was great joy in Rome. There was good news from Cincinnatus. The men of the mountains had been beaten with great loss. They had been driven back into their own place.

And now the Roman army, with the boys and the guards, was coming home with **banners**[1] flying, and shouts of victory; and at their head rode Cincinnatus. He had saved Rome.

Cincinnatus might then have made himself king; for his word was law, and no man dared lift a finger against him. But, before the people could thank him enough for what he had done, he gave back the power to the white-haired Roman Fathers, and went again to his little farm and his plow.

He had been the ruler of Rome for sixteen days.

辛辛那图斯把守城的卫兵和男孩子武装起来后，一马当先带领他们去攻打那些凶猛的山里人，解救已经陷入重围的罗马军队。

几天之后，罗马城举城欢庆。辛辛那图斯传来好消息，那些山里人遭到了重创，被赶了回去。

现在，罗马军队和守城的卫兵以及那些男孩子一起挥舞着旗帜，高喊着胜利的口号凯旋。辛辛那图斯骑马走在队伍的最前面，正是他拯救了整个罗马城。

辛辛那图斯原本可以成为国王，因为他说的话就是法律，也没有人敢出来反对他。可就在人人对他感恩戴德之时，辛辛那图斯却把权力重新移交给白发元老们，自己又回到小农庄种地去了。

辛辛那图斯一共只做了十六天的罗马统帅。

① banner ['bænə] n. 旗帜

25. The Story of Regulus

On the other side of the sea from Rome there was once a great city named **Carthage**[1]. The Roman people were never very friendly to the people of Carthage, and at last a war began between them. For a long time it was hard to tell which would prove the stronger. First the Romans would gain a battle, and then the men of Carthage would gain a battle; and so the war went on for many years.

Among the Romans there was a brave general named Regulus,—a man of whom it was said that he never **broke his word**[2]. It so happened after a while, that Regulus was taken **prisoner**[3] and carried to Carthage. Ill and very lonely, he dreamed of his wife and little children so far away beyond the sea; and he had but little hope of ever seeing them again. He loved his home **dearly**[4], but he believed that his first duty was to his country; and so he had left all, to fight in this **cruel**[5] war.

He had lost a battle, it is true, and had been taken prisoner. Yet he knew that the Romans were gaining ground, and the people of Carthage were afraid of being beaten in the end. They had sent into other countries to hire soldiers to help them; but even with these they would not be able to fight much longer against Rome.

One day some of the rulers of Carthage came to the prison to talk with Regulus.

"We should like to **make peace with**[6] the Roman people," they said, "and

25. 雷古鲁斯的故事

① Carthage ['kɑ:θidʒ] n. 迦太基（古代北非奴隶制国家，在今突尼斯境内，公元前146年被罗马所灭）

② break one's word 违背某人自己的诺言

③ prisoner ['prizənə] n. 囚犯，俘虏

④ dearly ['diəli] ad. 很，非常；充满深情地

⑤ cruel ['kru:əl] a. 残酷的

⑥ make peace with 与……讲和，休战

从前，有一个叫迦太基的大城市与罗马城隔海相望。罗马人对迦太基人一直心存芥蒂，最后双方爆发了一场战争。这场争斗持续了很多年，很难分出谁胜谁负，即便罗马人今天打赢了一场战役，迦太基人可能马上就会还以颜色。

罗马人里面有一个勇敢的将军名叫雷古鲁斯，人们说他是一个从不违背诺言的人。战争开始后不久，雷古鲁斯将军被俘，敌人把他送往迦太基关押起来。在疾病和极度孤独之中，雷古鲁斯将军梦见了远在大海对岸的妻子和孩子，可是再见到亲人的希望实在太渺茫了。雷古鲁斯深爱着他的家人，但是他认为自己的首要职责是为国家效力，因此他不顾一切地投入到这场残酷的战争之中。

雷古鲁斯吃了败仗，这是事实，而且还被敌人俘虏。但是他知道，罗马人的形势正在一天天地好转起来。由于害怕被罗马人打败，迦太基人已经派人去国外招募雇佣兵。但即便这样，在这场跟罗马人的战争中，他们已经坚持不了多长时间。

一天，迦太基的几个掌权者来到监牢与雷古鲁斯谈话。"我们有意与罗马人握手言和，"这几个人说，"我

· 137 ·

we are sure, that, if your rulers at home knew how the war is going, they would be glad to make peace with us. We will set you free and let you go home, if you will agree to do as we say."

"What is that?" asked Regulus.

"In the first place," they said, "you must tell the Romans about the battles which you have lost, and you must make it plain to them that they have not gained anything by the war. In the second place, you must promise us, that, if they will not make peace, you will come back to your prison."

"Very well," said Regulus, "I promise you, that, if they will not make peace, I will come back to prison."

And so they let him go; for they knew that a great Roman would **keep his word**①.

When he came to Rome, all the people greeted him gladly. His wife and children were very happy, for they thought that now they would not be parted again. The white-haired Fathers who made the laws for the city came to see him. They asked him about the war.

"I was sent from Carthage to ask you to make peace," he said. "But it will not be wise to make peace. True, we have been beaten in a few battles, but our army is gaining ground every day. The people of Carthage are afraid, and well they may be. Keep on with the war a little while longer, and Carthage shall be yours. **As for**② me, I have come to bid my wife and children and Rome farewell. Tomorrow I will start back to Carthage and to prison; for I have promised."

Then the Fathers tried to **persuade**③ him to stay.

"Let us send another man in your place," they said.

"Shall a Roman not keep his word?" answered Regulus. "I am ill, and at the best have not long to live. I will go back, as I promised."

His wife and little children wept, and his sons begged him not to leave them again.

们相信如果你们国内的掌权者知道了战争的形势,他们会很高兴和我们讲和的。如果你愿意照我们说的那样做,你就会获得自由,我们将放你回家。"

"那到底该怎么做?"雷古鲁斯问。

"首先,"他们说,"你要告诉罗马人你们所吃的败仗,同时要让他们明白,在战争中他们没有捞到任何好处。其次,你要向我们保证,如果罗马人拒绝讲和,你仍旧要回到牢房里面来。"

"好吧!"雷古鲁斯说,"我答应你们,如果他们拒绝讲和,我就重新回到牢房里面。"

于是迦太基人释放了雷古鲁斯,他们知道一个真正的罗马人是一定会信守诺言的。雷古鲁斯回到了罗马,所有人都兴高采烈地来迎接他。他的妻子和孩子见到他十分高兴,还以为从今天起就再也不分开了。掌管法律的白发元老们也前来探望他,询问有关战争的情况。

"迦太基人派我回来跟你们讲和。"雷古鲁斯说,"可是对于我们而言,现在谈和并不明智。的确,我们输掉了几次战役,但是我们的军队正在逐渐壮大。迦太基人心里害怕,也难怪他们害怕。如果战争继续打下去,要不了多久迦太基就是你们的囊中之物。至于我,我是回来跟妻儿和罗马告别的。明天我就要起身返回迦太基,回到牢房里去,我已经对他们作出了承诺。"

元老们都竭力劝他留下来不要回去。

"我们另派一个人去代替你!"他们说。

"身为罗马人,我怎么能够违背诺言?"雷古鲁斯说,"我病了,也活不了多长时间,我情愿回去履行我的诺言。"

妻子和年幼的孩子们都哭了起来,儿子们乞求他不要再离开他们。

① keep one's word 信守某人自己的诺言

② as for 至于,就……方面而言

③ persuade [pə'sweid] v. 说服(某人)做某事,恳求

"I have given my word," said Regulus. "The rest will be taken care of."

Then he bade them goodbye, and went bravely back to the prison and the cruel death which he expected.

This was the kind of courage that made Rome the greatest city in the world.

"我已经许下诺言。"雷古鲁斯说,"剩下的就由不得我了。"

最后,雷古鲁斯告别亲人,毅然回到牢房里面,他知道等待他的将是残酷的死亡。

也正是凭借着这种勇气,罗马才成为世界上最伟大的城市。

26. Cornelia's Jewels

It was a bright morning in the old city of Rome many hundred years ago. In a vine-covered summerhouse in a beautiful garden, two boys were standing. They were looking at their mother and her friend, who were walking among the flowers and trees.

"Did you ever see so handsome a lady as our mother's friend?" asked the younger boy, holding his tall brother's hand. "She looks like a queen."

"Yet she is not so beautiful as our mother," said the elder boy. "She has a fine dress, it is true; but her face is not noble and kind. It is our mother who is like a queen."

"That is true," said the other. "There is no woman in Rome so much like a queen as our own dear mother."

Soon Cornelia, their mother, came down the walk to speak with them. She was simply dressed in a plain white robe. Her arms and feet were bare, as was the custom in those days; and no rings nor chains glittered about her hands and neck. For her only crown, long **braids**[1] of soft brown hair were **coiled**[2] about her head; and a tender smile lit up her noble face as she looked into her sons' proud eyes.

"Boys," she said, "I have something to tell you."

They bowed before her, as Roman lads were taught to do, and said, "What is it, mother?"

26. 科妮莉娅的珠宝

　　数百年前，一个阳光明媚的早晨，在罗马古城一座美丽的花园里，两个小男孩站在一个爬满葡萄藤的凉亭里，望着母亲和她的朋友在花丛和树林中散步。

　　"你见没见过像母亲朋友那样漂亮的女士？"年纪小一点的男孩抓着高个子哥哥的手问："她看上去真像一个女王！"

　　"不过她还没有母亲漂亮呢！"哥哥说，"她衣着华贵，这不假，可是她的容貌并不高贵典雅，我们母亲才像一个女王。"

　　"是啊，"另一个孩子接着说，"罗马城没有一个女人比我们亲爱的母亲看起来更像女王了。"

　　过了一阵，男孩的母亲科妮莉娅走过来和他们说话。按照当时的习惯，她只穿了一件简单的白色长袍，手臂和脚都露在外面，手上没有戴戒指，脖子上也没有项链，仅有的皇冠便是盘在头顶上的棕色柔软长辫①。望着孩子眼中自豪的神情，温柔的笑容浮现在她高贵的脸上。

　　"孩子们，"她说，"我要给你们说一件事。"

　　两个男孩依照罗马的礼节向母亲鞠躬行礼，然后问："是什么事，母亲？"

---

① braid [breid] n. 发辫
② coil [kɔil] v. 盘绕

· 143 ·

"You are to dine with us today, here in the garden; and then our friend is going to show us that wonderful **casket**① of jewels of which you have heard so much."

The brothers looked shyly at their mother's friend. Was it possible that she had still other rings besides those on her fingers? Could she have other **gems**② besides those which sparkled in the chains about her neck?

When the simple outdoor meal was over, a servant brought the casket from the house. The lady opened it. Ah, how those jewels dazzled the eyes of the wondering boys! There were ropes of pearls, white as milk, and smooth as **satin**③; **heaps**④ of shining **rubies**⑤, red as the glowing coals; **sapphires**⑥ as blue as the sky that summer day; and diamonds that flashed and sparkled like the sunlight.

The brothers looked long at the gems.

"Ah!" whispered the younger; "if our mother could only have such beautiful things!"

At last, however, the casket was closed and carried carefully away.

"Is it true, Cornelia, that you have no jewels?" asked her friend. "Is it true, as I have heard it whispered, that you are poor?"

"No, I am not poor," answered Cornelia, and as she spoke she drew her two boys to her side; "for here are my jewels. They are worth more than all your gems."

I am sure that the boys never forgot their mother's pride and love and care; and in after years, when they had become great men in Rome, they often thought of this scene in the garden. And the world still likes to hear the story of Cornelia's jewels.

① casket ['kɑ:skit] n. 小匣子

② gem [dʒem] n. 珍宝

③ satin ['sætən] n. 缎子
④ heap [hi:p] n.（一）堆
⑤ ruby ['ru:bi] n. 红宝石
⑥ sapphire ['sæfaiə] n. 蓝宝石

"今天你们要和大人一起在花园里面用餐，我们的朋友将要展示那个你们已经听说过很多次的神奇珠宝箱。"

兄弟俩一脸腼腆地望着母亲的朋友，心想除了手上戴的那些戒指，她难道还有别的戒指？如果不算脖子上闪闪发光的项链，她难道还有其他宝石？

简单的室外餐会结束了。一个仆人从屋里面拿出一个珠宝箱，那位女士打开箱子。啊！兄弟俩惊奇地看着里面的珠宝，简直目不暇接！成串的珍珠像牛奶一样洁白，像绸缎一样丝滑；成堆的红宝石像燃烧的煤块闪闪发光；蓝宝石蓝得像夏日的天空；还有那些钻石，闪烁着太阳般的光芒。

兄弟俩凝视着那些珠宝许久许久。

"啊！"弟弟低声说，"如果母亲也有这些漂亮的东西该多好啊！"

珠宝箱的盖子合上后，被小心翼翼地拿走了。

"科妮莉娅，你没有珠宝，这是真的吗？"她的朋友问，"我听人私下里说你很穷，这是不是真的？"

"不，我并不穷。"科妮莉娅一边回答，一边把两个孩子拉到身旁，"这就是我的珠宝，他们比你所有宝石的价值还要高。"

我深信，那两个孩子将永远不会忘记母亲为他们流露出来的骄傲、热爱和关切之情。许多年后，两兄弟成为罗马城了不起的大人物，他们还时常会想起发生在花园里的那一幕。世界上的人也依然很喜欢听到有关科妮莉娅珠宝的故事。

145

27. Androclus and the Lion

In Rome there was once a poor slave whose name was Androclus. His master was a cruel man, and so unkind to him that at last Androclus ran away.

He hid himself in a wild wood for many days; but there was no food to be found, and he grew so weak and sick that he thought he should die. So one day he crept into a cave and lay down, and soon he was fast asleep.

After a while a great noise woke him up. A lion had come into the cave, and was roaring loudly. Androclus was very much afraid, for he felt sure that the beast would kill him. Soon, however, he saw that the lion was not angry, but that he **limped**[1] as though his foot hurt him.

Then Androclus grew so bold that he took hold of the lion's lame paw to see what was the matter. The lion stood quite still, and rubbed his head against the man's shoulder. He seemed to say,—

"I know that you will help me."

Androclus lifted the paw from the ground, and saw that it was a long, sharp **thorn**[2] which hurt the lion so much. He took the end of the thorn in his fingers; then he gave a strong, quick pull, and out it came. The lion was full of joy. He jumped about like a dog, and **licked**[3] the hands and feet of his new friend.

27. 安德洛克鲁斯和狮子

　　从前，罗马有一个可怜的奴隶名叫安德洛克鲁斯，他的主人是一个狠心的家伙，对他十分恶毒。迫不得已，安德洛克鲁斯只好逃走了。

　　安德洛克鲁斯跑到原始森林里藏了很多天。由于缺少食物，身体日渐病弱，安德洛克鲁斯担心自己不久可能就要离开人世。有一天，他爬到一个山洞里面，躺下后很快就睡着了。

　　没过多久，他被一阵巨大的声响吵醒了。原来是一头狮子爬进了山洞，大声地咆哮着。安德洛克鲁斯感到十分害怕，担心野兽会把他吃掉。可是他很快发现，狮子并没有发怒，原来它的一只脚瘸着，好像受了伤。

　　安德洛克鲁斯的胆子大了起来，他抓起狮子的脚查看伤情。狮子安静地蹲在那里，头直往他的肩膀上蹭，似乎在说：

　　"我知道你会帮助我的。"

　　安德洛克鲁斯把狮子的脚从地上抬起来，发现里面扎着一根长长的利刺，便用手捏住刺一使劲，一下子拔了出来。狮子高兴极了，像狗一样跳起来舔这个新朋友的手和脚。

① limp [limp] v. 跛行

② thorn [θɔːn] n. 刺

③ lick [lik] v. 舔

Androclus was not at all afraid after this; and when night came, he and the lion lay down and slept side by side.

For a long time, the lion brought food to Androclus every day; and the two became such good friends, that Androclus found his new life a very happy one.

One day some soldiers who were passing through the wood found Androclus in the cave. They knew who he was, and so took him back to Rome.

It was the law at that time that every slave who ran away from his master should be made to fight a hungry lion. So a fierce lion was shut up for a while without food, and a time was set for the fight.

When the day came, thousands of people crowded to see the sport. They went to such places at that time very much as people nowadays go to see a circus show or a game of baseball.

The door opened, and poor Androclus was brought in. He was almost dead with fear, for the roars of the lion could already be heard. He looked up, and saw that there was no pity in the thousands of faces around him.

Then the hungry lion rushed in. With a single **bound**① he reached the poor slave. Androclus gave a great cry, not of fear, but of gladness. It was his old friend, the lion of the cave.

The people, who had expected to see the man killed by the lion, were filled with **wonder**②. They saw Androclus put his arms around the lion's neck; they saw the lion lie down at his feet, and lick them lovingly; they saw the great beast rub his head against the slave's face as though he wanted to be petted. They could not understand what it all meant.

After a while they asked Androclus to tell them about it. So he stood up before them, and, with his arm around the lion's neck, told how he and the beast had lived together in the cave.

"I am a man," he said; "but no man has ever befriended me. This poor lion alone has been kind to me; and we love each other as brothers."

从那以后，安德洛克鲁斯不再感到害怕了，晚上还和狮子靠在一起睡觉。

日子就这样一天天地过去了，狮子每天都会带些食物回来给安德洛克鲁斯吃，他们两个成为非常要好的朋友。对于这种新的生活，安德洛克鲁斯也觉得十分快乐。

一天，几个士兵从森林里面经过，在山洞里面发现了安德洛克鲁斯。他们知道安德洛克鲁斯是谁，于是便把他带回了罗马城。

按照当时的法律规定，凡是从主人那里逃走的奴隶，都要和一只饥饿的狮子搏斗。一旦搏斗的日子确定下来，一只凶猛的狮子就要被关起来饿上几天。

当天，成千上万的人涌来观看这场搏斗，当时看搏斗对于他们而言，就像我们今天去看马戏表演或棒球赛一样。

门打开了，可怜的安德洛克鲁斯被带了进来，听到狮子的咆哮声，他差一点没被吓死。抬头望去，他看见几千名围观者的脸上没有一丝怜悯。

紧接着，那只饥饿的狮子冲了进来，一下子跳到这个可怜的奴隶面前。安德洛克鲁斯大喊了一声，不过不是因为恐惧，而是因为太兴奋了。原来这只狮子正是他的老朋友，是山洞里面的那只狮子呀！

那些盼着看他被狮子咬死的观众心里都充满了疑惑。他们看见安德洛克鲁斯伸出手搂住狮子，又看见狮子躺在他脚下深情地舔着他的脚。他们还看见这只巨兽用自己的头蹭着奴隶的脸，好像要得到他的宠爱似的，他们不明白这到底是怎么回事。

片刻之后，他们询问安德洛克鲁斯。安德洛克鲁斯站了起来，胳膊依然搂在狮子的脖子上，他向大家讲述了他和这头野兽在山洞里一起生活的故事。

"我是人。"他说，"可是从来没有人对我好过，只有这只可怜的狮子，待我像亲兄弟一样。"

Androclus and the Lion

The people were not so bad that they could be cruel to the poor slave now. "Live and be free!" they cried. "Live and be free!"

Others cried, "Let the lion go free too! Give both of them their liberty!"

And so Androclus was set free, and the lion was given to him for his own. And they lived together in Rome for many years.

① bound [baʊnd] *n.* 跳跃

② wonder ['wʌndə] *n.* 惊愕

安德洛克鲁斯和狮子

　　那些围观者的良知并没有泯灭，觉得不能再这样残酷对待这个可怜的奴隶。"饶他一命，给他自由！"他们一起不停地喊着。

　　其他人也跟着喊了起来，"把狮子也放了！给他们自由！"

　　于是，安德洛克鲁斯被释放了，那只狮子也归他所有，他们一起在罗马生活了很多年。

28. Horatius at the Bridge

Once there was a war between the Roman people and the **Etruscans**[1] who lived in the towns on the other side of the Tiber River. Porsena, the King of the Etruscans, raised a great army, and marched toward Rome. The city had never been in so great danger.

The Romans did not have very many fighting men at that time, and they knew that they were not strong enough to meet the Etruscans in open battle. So they kept themselves inside of their walls, and set guards to watch the roads.

One morning the army of Porsena was seen coming over the hills from the north. There were thousands of horsemen and footmen, and they were marching straight toward the wooden bridge which spanned the river at Rome.

"What shall we do?" said the white-haired Fathers who made the laws for the Roman people. "If they once gain the bridge, we cannot **hinder**[2] them from crossing; and then what hope will there be for the town?"

Now, among the guards at the bridge, there was a brave man named Horatius. He was on the farther side of the river, and when he saw that the Etruscans were so near, he called out to the Romans who were behind him.

"**Hew**[3] down the bridge with all the speed that you can!" he cried. "I, with the two men who stand by me, will **keep the foe at bay**[4]."

Then, with their shields before them, and their long spears in their hands, the

28. 桥上的贺雷修斯

① Etruscan [iˈtrʌskən] n. 伊特鲁里亚人

从前，罗马人和住在台伯河对岸的伊特鲁里亚人之间发生了一场战争。伊特鲁里亚的国王波西那召集大队人马向罗马进军，罗马城处于前所未有的危机之中。

当时，罗马城里英勇善战的战士并不多，罗马人知道自己还没有足够的实力与伊特鲁里亚人进行正面交战。于是，他们坚守在城内，并且派卫兵去把守要道。

一天早晨，罗马人看见波西那的军队从北面翻山打过来，数千名骑兵和步兵一起，径直向罗马城外台伯河上的那座木桥冲来。

"我们该怎么办？"掌管罗马法律的白发元老们说，"一旦让他们占领了那座桥，我们就无法阻止他们过桥，罗马城就没有希望了。"

② hinder [ˈhində] v. 阻碍

当时，守桥的士兵中有一名勇士叫贺雷修斯。贺雷修斯一直坚守在台伯河的对岸，看到伊特鲁里亚人已经逼近，便向身后的罗马人大声喊着。

"快以最快的速度把桥砍断！"贺雷修斯叫道，"我，还有我身边的两个人一起去把敌人拦住。"

③ hew [hju:] v. 砍倒
④ keep...at bay 使无法近身

说完，三个人把盾牌放在胸前，手持长矛，勇敢地

· 153 ·

three brave men stood in the road, and kept back the horsemen whom Porsena had sent to take the bridge.

On the bridge the Romans hewed away at the beams and posts. Their axes rang, the chips flew fast; and soon it trembled, and was ready to fall.

"Come back! come back, and save your lives!" they cried to Horatius and the two who were with him.

But just then Porsena's horsemen dashed toward them again.

"Run for your lives!" said Horatius to his friends. "I will keep the road."

They turned, and ran back across the bridge. They had hardly reached the other side when there was a crashing of beams and **timbers**①. The bridge **toppled**② over to one side, and then fell with a great **splash**③ into the water.

When Horatius heard the sound, he knew that the city was safe. With his face still toward Porsena's men, he moved slowly backward till he stood on the river's bank. A **dart**④ thrown by one of Porsena's soldiers put out his left eye; but he did not **falter**⑤. He cast his spear at the fore-most horseman, and then he turned quickly around. He saw the white porch of his own home among the trees on the other side of the stream;

> "And he spake to the noble river
>   That rolls by the walls of Rome:
> 'O Tiber! father Tiber!
>   To whom the Romans pray,
> A Roman's life, a Roman's arms,
>   Take thou in charge today.'"

He leaped into the deep, swift stream. He still had his heavy armor on; and when he sank out of sight, no one thought that he would ever be seen again. But he was a strong man, and the best swimmer in Rome. The next minute he rose. He was halfway across the river, and safe from the spears and darts which Porsena's soldiers **hurled**⑥ after him.

① timber ['timbə] *n.* 木料
② topple ['tɔpl] *v.* 倾倒
③ splash [splæʃ] *n.* 飞溅的水

④ dart [dɑ:t] *n.* 标枪
⑤ falter ['fɔ:ltə] *v.* 动摇，畏缩

⑥ hurl [hə:l] *v.* 用力投掷

站在道路的中间，把波西那派来攻桥的骑兵挡在那里。

桥上的罗马人正在飞快砍着桥梁和桥柱。他们挥舞着斧头，木头的碎片纷纷落下。一转眼间，桥便开始摇摇欲坠起来，眼看就要倒下去。

"赶快朝回跑！赶快！不然就没命了！"罗马人向贺雷修斯和另外两个人喊道。

可就在那时，波西那的骑兵再度冲了过来。

"你们快往回跑！"贺雷修斯对他的朋友们说，"我来挡住他们。"

那两个士兵转身就向桥的另一头跑去。就在他们刚刚到达河对岸的一刹那，桥梁和桥柱突然倒向了一边，随即落入水中，溅起了巨大的波浪。

贺雷修斯听到这声响，知道罗马城已经安全了，而他依然面朝波西那的士兵，慢慢后退到河岸边上。突然，一个波西那的士兵掷出标枪，正中贺雷修斯的左眼，可是他并没有倒下。贺雷修斯把长矛投向冲在队伍最前面的骑兵，然后迅速转身，望了一眼河对岸树林里自己家的白色门廊。

"他向环绕罗马城神圣的河祈祷：
'啊，台伯！台伯我父！
罗马人向你祈祷，
一个罗马人的性命，
一个罗马人的武器，
今天全都托付给你了！'"

说完，贺雷修斯纵身跳进水深流急的河中，连同身上厚重的盔甲一起慢慢消失在人们的视线中，没有人会想到他还会生还。可是贺雷修斯身体强壮，是罗马城最好的游泳能手。他再次在河水中出现的时候，已经游到

· 155 ·

Soon he reached the farther side, where his friends stood ready to help him. Shout after shout greeted him as he climbed upon the bank. Then Porsena's men shouted also, for they had never seen a man so brave and strong as Horatius. He had kept them out of Rome, but he had done a deed which they could not help but praise.

As for the Romans, they were very grateful to Horatius for having saved their city. They called him Horatius Co′cles, which meant the "one-eyed Horatius," because he had lost an eye in defending the bridge; they caused a fine statue of brass to be made in his honor; and they gave him as much land as he could plow around in a day. And for hundreds of years afterwards—

> "With weeping and with laughter,
>   Still was the story told,
> How well Horatius kept the bridge
>   In the brave days of old."

台伯河的中央,到了波西那的士兵扔过来的长矛和标枪射程之外。

很快,贺雷修斯游到了河对岸,朋友们早已站在那里准备接应他。他爬上河岸,耳朵里响起人们一阵又一阵的欢呼声,紧接着就听见河对岸波西那的士兵们也高呼了起来。原来他们从未见过像贺雷修斯这样勇敢坚强的人,虽然贺雷修斯把他们挡在罗马城外,可是他的英勇事迹却让人肃然起敬。

罗马人为了感谢贺雷修斯挽救了他们的城市,称他为"贺雷修斯·科克拉斯",意思是"独眼的贺雷修斯",因为他为了守卫大桥失去了一只眼睛。为了纪念贺雷修斯的英勇事迹,他们还雕刻了一座精美的铜像,送给他很多土地,他一个人要一天才能犁完。数百年后:

"有泪水也有欢笑,
那个故事依然这样传唱,
贺雷修斯英勇保卫那座桥,
在那英勇无畏的过往。"

29. Julius Cæsar

Nearly two thousand years ago there lived in Rome a man whose name was Julius Cæsar. He was the greatest of all the Romans.

Why was he so great?

He was a brave warrior, and had conquered many countries for Rome. He was wise in planning and in doing. He knew how to make men both love and fear him.

At last he made himself the ruler of Rome. Some said that he wished to become its king. But the Romans at that time did not believe in kings.

Once when Cæsar was passing through a little country village, all the men, women, and children of the place came out to see him. There were not more than fifty of them, all together, and they were led by their mayor, who told each one what to do.

These simple people stood by the roadside and watched Cæsar pass. The mayor looked very proud and happy; for was he not the ruler of this village? He felt that he was almost as great a man as Cæsar himself.

Some of the fine officers who were with Cæsar laughed. They said, "See how that fellow struts at the head of his little flock!"

"Laugh as you will," said Cæsar, "he has reason to be proud. I would rather be the head man of a village than the second man in Rome!"

29. 尤利乌斯·恺撒

大约两千年前，有一个名叫尤利乌斯·恺撒的罗马人，是全罗马城最伟大的人。

那么尤利乌斯·恺撒究竟为什么如此伟大？

因为他骁勇善战，为罗马征服了很多国家；他智谋过人，行事老练，懂得怎样使自己的子民敬畏他。

最后，恺撒成为罗马最高的掌权者。有人说他想做罗马国王，可是当时的罗马人并不相信君主制度。

一次，恺撒经过一个小村庄。全村男女老少加起来还不到五十人，他们在村长的带领下出来迎接恺撒。村长吩咐每个人具体都要做些什么。

这些纯朴的村民站在路旁，注视着恺撒从这里经过。村长看上去是那么自豪又那么快乐，难道他不正是全村最高的统治者吗？因此，村长觉得自己和恺撒本人几乎一样伟大。

几个跟随恺撒的高官们看见后都笑了起来。他们说："你们看那个家伙！他率领着那一小撮人，显得那么洋洋自得！"

"随你们怎么嘲笑！"恺撒说，"他有理由感到骄傲。

At another time, Cæsar was crossing a narrow sea in a boat. Before he was halfway to the farther shore, a storm **overtook**① him. The wind blew hard; the waves dashed high; the lightning **flashed**②; the thunder **rolled**③.

It seemed every minute as though the boat would sink. The captain was in great fright. He had crossed the sea many times, but never in such a storm as this. He trembled with fear; he could not guide the boat; he fell down upon his knees; he **moaned**④, "All is lost! all is lost!"

But Cæsar was not afraid. He bade the man get up and take his oars again.

"Why should you be afraid?" he said. "The boat will not be lost; for you have Cæsar on board."

我倒宁愿做一个村的村长，也不愿意做罗马的第二号人物。"

还有一次，恺撒乘船经过一片狭窄的海域。船刚刚行驶到一半的距离，风暴突然向他袭来。狂风猛烈地吹着，掀起汹涌的海浪，天空中电光闪烁，雷声隆隆。

那艘船看起来似乎随时都有沉没的可能，船长心里感到十分害怕。虽然他已经横渡大海很多次，可还从来没有见过像今天这样的风浪。他吓得全身哆嗦着，根本无法指挥船的航行。船长双膝跪地，嘴里喃喃地说着："完了！全完了！"

可是恺撒丝毫没有感到害怕，他命令船长站起来重新拿起船桨。

"你为什么要害怕？"他说，"有我恺撒在，船就永远不会沉没！"

① overtook [ˌəuvəˈtuk] v. (overtake 的过去式) 突然降临于
② flash [flæʃ] v. 闪光
③ roll [rəul] v. (雷、鼓等) 发出隆隆声
④ moan [məun] v. 悲叹

30. The Sword of Damocles

There was once a king whose name was Dionysius. He was so unjust and cruel that he won for himself the name of tyrant. He knew that almost everybody hated him, and so he was always in **dread**① **lest**② some one should take his life.

But he was very rich, and he lived in a fine palace where there were many beautiful and costly things, and he was waited upon by a host of servants who were always ready to **do his bidding**③. One day a friend of his, whose name was Damocles, said to him,—

"How happy you must be! You have here everything that any man could wish."

"Perhaps you would like to change places with me," said the tyrant.

"No, not that, O king!" said Damocles; "but I think, that, if I could only have your riches and your pleasures for one day, I should not want any greater happiness."

"Very well," said the tyrant. "You shall have them."

And so, the next day, Damocles was led into the palace, and all the servants were bidden to treat him as their master. He sat down at a table in the banquet hall, and rich foods were placed before him.

Nothing was wanting that could give him pleasure. There were costly wines, and beautiful flowers, and rare perfumes, and delightful music. He

30. 达摩克利斯之剑

① dread [dred] *n*. 恐惧，畏惧；令人恐惧的事物
② lest [lest] *conj*. 以免；唯恐；生怕
③ do sb.'s bidding 照某人命令办事

  从前，有一个国王名叫狄奥尼修斯，此人十分残忍邪恶，所以大家都称他暴君。国王知道几乎所有人都憎恨他，因此每天总是惶惶不可终日，害怕有人来取他的性命。
  狄奥尼修斯非常富有，住在一座豪华的宫殿里面，那里奇珍异石应有尽有，身旁还有一大群仆人随时听候他的调遣。一天，有一个名叫达摩克利斯的朋友对他说：
  "你一定过得十分快活，你拥有所有人都向往的东西。"
  "你是不是想和我交换一下位置？"暴君问。
  "不不，国王陛下，我不是那个意思！"达摩克利斯说，"我想如果我能拥有像您一样的财富和欢乐，哪怕只有一天时间，我也知足了。"
  "好吧！"暴君说，"我就满足你的愿望。"
  于是，第二天达摩克利斯被带到宫里，国王要求所有仆人要像对待主人那样服侍他。达摩克利斯坐在宴会大厅的餐桌旁，面前摆满了丰盛的食物。
  现在，能让达摩克利斯快乐的东西一样都不缺：名贵的美酒、美丽的鲜花、稀有的香水，还有悦耳的音

rested himself among soft **cushions**①, and felt that he was the happiest man in all the world.

Then he chanced to raise his eyes toward the ceiling. What was it that was dangling above him, with its point almost touching his head? It was a sharp sword, and it was hung by only a single horse-hair. What if the hair should break? There was danger every moment that it would do so.

The Sword of Damocles

The smile **faded**② from the lips of Damocles. His face became ashy pale. His hands trembled. He wanted no more food; he could drink no more wine; he took no more delight in the music. He longed to be out of the palace, and away, he cared not where.

"What is the matter?" said the tyrant.

"That sword! that sword!" cried Damocles. He was so badly frightened that he dared not move.

① cushion ['kuʃən] n. 垫子

乐。他靠在柔软的垫子上面，觉得自己是世界上最快乐的人。

　　达摩克利斯无意间抬头望见了天花板，发现头顶上有个东西正在晃来晃去，尖的地方还差点碰到他的头上。原来那是一把锋利的宝剑，仅靠一根马鬃绑着挂在那里。假如马鬃断了，将会产生怎样的后果？马鬃随时都有断掉的可能，宝剑也有随时落下来的危险。

达摩克利斯之剑

② fade [feid] v. 逐渐消失

　　一刹那间，笑容从达摩克利斯的嘴角消失了，他的脸色变得十分苍白，双手也开始颤抖起来。他再也不想什么美食和美酒了，也再没有心思去欣赏音乐了，一心一意只想快点离开这个宫殿，跑得远远的，不管去哪里都行。

　　"你怎么了？"暴君问。

　　"那把剑！那把剑！"达摩克利斯叫着，差一点要被吓死，坐在那里一动也不敢动。

"Yes," said Dionysius, "I know there is a sword above your head, and that it may fall at any moment. But why should that trouble you? I have a sword over my head all the time. I am every moment in dread lest something may cause me to lose my life."

"Let me go," said Damocles. "I now see that I was mistaken, and that the rich and powerful are not so happy as they seem. Let me go back to my old home in the poor little cottage among the mountains."

And so long as he lived, he never again wanted to be rich, or to change places, even for a moment, with the king.

"是啊！"狄奥尼修斯说，"我知道你头顶上有把剑。这把剑随时都有掉下来的可能，可是你为什么如此烦恼不安呢？我的头顶上无论什么时候都有一把剑，我无时无刻不在担心会有什么东西要我的命。"

　　"放我走吧！"达摩克利斯哀求道，"现在我知道自己错了，那些有权有钱的人其实并不像他们看起来那么快活，还是让我回到山中破旧的小屋去吧！"

　　在有生之年，达摩克利斯再也不想成为富翁，也不想跟国王交换位置，即便一分一秒都不行。

31. Damon and Pythias

A young man whose name was Pythias had done something which the tyrant Dionysius did not like. For this offense he was dragged to prison, and a day was set when he should be put to death. His home was far away, and he wanted very much to see his father and mother and friends before he died.

"Only give me leave to go home and say goodbye to those whom I love," he said, "and then I will come back and give up my life."

The tyrant laughed at him.

"How can I know that you will keep your promise?" he said. "You only want to cheat me, and save yourself."

Then a young man whose name was Damon spoke and said,—

"O king! put me in prison in place of my friend Pythias, and let him go to his own country to put his affairs in order, and to bid his friends **farewell**[1]. I know that he will come back as he promised, for he is a man who has never broken his word. But if he is not here on the day which you have set, then I will die **in his stead**[2]."

The tyrant was surprised that anybody should make such an offer. He at last agreed to let Pythias go, and gave orders that the young man Damon should be shut up in prison.

Time passed, and by and by the day drew near which had been set for Pythias

31. 达蒙和皮西厄斯

有一个名叫皮西厄斯的年轻人，做了一些让暴君狄奥尼修斯厌恶的事情，由于这个罪名他被捕入狱，执行死刑的日期已经确定了下来。皮西厄斯的家离这里很远，他渴望在临死前能再见父母和朋友们一面。

"我唯一的愿望是让我回去和那些亲爱的人告别。"他说，"回来之后，我就去受死。"

暴君对他大笑了起来。

"我怎么知道你会不会信守诺言？"他说，"你不过是骗我，想救自己的命罢了。"

这时，一个名叫达蒙的年轻人向国王求情。他说："国王陛下，把我关进监狱代替我的朋友皮西厄斯，让他回家安排后事跟朋友们告别。我知道皮西厄斯一定会信守诺言，如果到时间他没有回来，我愿意代他受死。"

竟然还有人这样求情，暴君感到非常吃惊。最终他同意让皮西厄斯回家，下令把达蒙关进监狱。

时光飞逝。执行死刑的日期一天天临近了，可是皮

① farewell ['fɛə'wel] n. 告别
② in one's stead 代替某人

to die; and he had not come back. The tyrant ordered the **jailer**① to keep close watch upon Damon, and not let him escape. But Damon did not try to escape. He still had faith in the truth and honor of his friend. He said, "If Pythias does not come back in time, it will not be his fault. It will be because he is hindered against his will."

At last the day came, and then the very hour. Damon was ready to die. His trust in his friend was as firm as ever; and he said that he did not grieve at having to suffer for one whom he loved so much.

Then the jailer came to lead him to his death; but at the same moment Pythias stood in the door. He had been delayed by storms and shipwreck, and he had feared that he was too late. He greeted Damon kindly, and then gave himself into the hands of the jailer. He was happy because he thought that he had come in time, even though it was at the last moment.

The tyrant was not so bad but that he could see good in others. He felt that men who loved and trusted each other, as did Damon and Pythias, ought not to suffer unjustly. And so he set them both free.

"I would give all my wealth to have one such friend," he said.

① jailer ['dʒeilə(r)] *n.* 狱卒

西厄斯还不见踪影。暴君命令狱卒对达蒙严加看守，以防止他逃跑。可是达蒙并不想逃跑，他依然相信朋友的诚实和道义。他说："如果皮西厄斯未能及时赶回来，那不是他的错，一定是有什么事情耽搁了。"

执行死刑的那一天终于到了，行刑的最后时刻也来到了。达蒙已经做好了赴死的准备，但是他对朋友的信念依然没有改变。他说为了一个深爱的人去死，自己不会感到难过。

于是，狱卒进来准备带达蒙去执行死刑。可就在那时，皮西厄斯出现在监狱的门口。他乘坐的船在暴风雨中沉没，延误了他的归程，他生怕自己不能按时赶回来。皮西厄斯亲切地跟达蒙打过招呼，把自己交到狱卒手上。皮西厄斯十分庆幸在行刑前的最后时刻，自己终于赶了回来。

这个暴君的心还没有坏透，还能够看到别人身上的好品德。他觉得像达蒙和皮西厄斯这样互相爱护互相信赖的人，不应该遭到这样不公正的处决，于是便下令把两人都放了。

国王说："假如能得到这样一个朋友，我愿意用全部财富去交换。"

32. A Laconic Answer

Many miles beyond Rome there was a famous country which we call Greece. The people of Greece were not united like the Romans; but instead there were several states, each of which had its own rulers.

Some of the people in the southern part of the country were called Spartans, and they were noted for their simple habits and their bravery. The name of their land was Laconia, and so they were sometimes called Lacons.

One of the strange rules which the Spartans had, was that they should speak briefly, and never use more words than were needed. And so a short answer is often spoken of as being laconic; that is, as being such an answer as a Lacon would be likely to give.

There was in the northern part of Greece a land called Macedon; and this land was at one time ruled over by a war-like king named Philip.

Philip of Macedon wanted to become the master of all Greece. So he raised a great army, and made war upon the other states, until nearly all of them were forced to call him their king. Then he sent a letter to the Spartans in Laconia, and said, "If I go down into your country, I will level your great city to the ground."

In a few days, an answer was brought back to him. When he opened the letter, he found only one word written there.

32．简洁的回答

离罗马很远的地方是著名的国家希腊，可是希腊人并不像罗马人那样团结一心，他们分裂成为很多小的城邦，每个城邦都有自己的统治者。

希腊的南部生活着斯巴达人，这些人因为生活简朴和勇敢无畏而著称于世。他们住在一个叫拉科尼亚的地方，所以有时候人们也称他们为拉科尼亚人。

斯巴达人有一条奇怪的规定，要求人们讲话必须简洁，不允许多说一个字。因此，一个简短的回答也常常被称为"拉科尼可"，意思是说这样的回答就像拉科尼亚人说话一样。

希腊北部有一个国家叫马其顿，这里曾经由好战的国王腓力统治。

马其顿的腓力国王想统治整个希腊，于是便纠集起大军与其他城邦交战，妄图迫使所有的城邦都臣服于他。一天，国王腓力给拉科尼亚的斯巴达人写了封信，信中这样写道："我如果进入你的国家，就要将你的城邦夷为平地。"

几天之后，腓力国王收到斯巴达人的回信。打开信封后，他发现信里面只写了一个词。

That word was "IF."

It was as much as to say, "We are not afraid of you so long as the little word 'if' stands in your way."

那个词就是"如果"。

这就相当于斯巴达人在说:"我们不怕你。'如果'有种,你们就来试试!"

33. The Ungrateful Guest

Among the soldiers of King Philip there was a poor man who had done some brave deeds. He had pleased the king in more ways than one, and so the king put a good deal of trust in him.

One day this soldier was on board of a ship at sea when a great storm came up. The winds drove the ship upon the rocks, and it was **wrecked**[①]. The soldier was cast half-drowned upon the shore; and he would have died there, had it not been for the kind care of a farmer who lived close by.

33. 忘恩负义的客人

腓力国王的士兵里面有一个穷人。此人曾经做过一些英勇的事迹，加之善于讨好国王，所以深得国王的信任。

一天，这个士兵乘船出海，在海上突然遭遇暴风雨的袭击，他乘坐的船触礁遇险，差一点送了命。海水将他冲到海岸上，幸亏得到附近一个农夫的悉心照顾，不然他可能就要死在那里。

① wreck [rek] v. 使失事

When the soldier was well enough to go home, he thanked the farmer for what he had done, and promised that he would repay him for his kindness.

But he did not mean to keep his promise. He did not tell King Philip about the man who had saved his life. He only said that there was a fine farm by the seashore, and that he would like very much to have it for his own. Would the king give it to him?

"Who owns the farm now?" asked Philip.

"Only a **churlish**① farmer, who has never done anything for his country," said the soldier.

"Very well, then," said Philip. "You have served me for a long time, and you shall have your wish. Go and take the farm for yourself."

And so the soldier made haste to drive the farmer from his house and home. He took the farm for his own.

The poor farmer was **stung**② to the heart by such treatment. He went boldly to the king, and told the whole story from beginning to end. King Philip was very angry when he learned that the man whom he had trusted had done so **base**③ a deed. He sent for the soldier in great haste; and when he had come, he caused these words to be burned in his forehead: —

"THE UNGRATEFUL GUEST."

Thus all the world was made to know of the **mean**④ act by which the soldier had tried to enrich himself; and from that day until he died all men **shunned**⑤ and hated him.

① churlish ['tʃɜːliʃ] *a.* 没有礼貌的

② stung [stʌŋ] *v.* 使疼痛（sting 的过去分词）

③ base [beis] *a.* 卑鄙的

④ mean [miːn] *a.* 卑鄙的
⑤ shun [ʃʌn] *v.* 躲开

士兵身体康复后打算回家。他感谢农夫为他所做的一切，并且承诺说将来一定要报答农夫的救命之恩。

可是士兵并不打算履行自己的诺言。他在向腓力国王汇报的时候，也没有提起那个救他性命的人，只说海边有一座非常好的农场，他很想要，问国王能不能把农场赏给他。

"那个农场现在的主人是谁？"腓力国王问。

"是一个粗鄙的农夫，他从来没有为国家出过什么力。"士兵说。

"那好！"腓力国王说，"你为我效力了这么长时间，我当然要满足你的这个愿望。就这样吧，那个农场归你了。"

于是，这个士兵去把农夫赶出家园，将农场据为己有。

可怜的农夫伤透了心，壮着胆子跑到国王那里，把事情的原委仔细说了一遍。国王得知自己信任的人竟然做出这种卑鄙的事情，大为震怒。他马上派人把那个士兵叫来，在他的额头上烙下这样几个字：

"忘恩负义的客人！"

就这样，世人都知道这个士兵为了满足自己的私欲，竟然干出如此卑鄙事情。从那一天起一直到他死去，所有人都躲着他，憎恨他。

34. Alexander and Bucephalus

One day King Philip bought a fine horse called Bucephalus. He was a noble animal, and the king paid a very high price for him. But he was wild and savage, and no man could **mount**[1] him, or do anything at all with him.

They tried to **whip**[2] him, but that only made him worse. At last the king bade his servants take him away.

"It is a pity to ruin so fine a horse as that," said Alexander, the king's young son. "Those men do not know how to treat him."

"Perhaps you can do better than they," said his father **scornfully**[3].

"I know," said Alexander, "that, if you would only give me leave to try, I could manage this horse better than any one else."

"And if you fail to do so, what then?" asked Philip.

"I will pay you the price of the horse," said the lad.

While everybody was laughing, Alexander ran up to Bucephalus, and turned his head toward the sun. He had noticed that the horse was afraid of his own shadow.

He then spoke gently to the horse, and **patted**[4] him with his hand. When he had quieted him a little, he made a quick **spring**[5], and leaped upon the horse's back.

34. 亚历山大和布西发拉斯

① mount [maunt] *v.* 骑上（马、自行车等）
② whip [hwip] *v.* 抽打

③ scornfully ['skɔːnfəli] *ad.* 轻蔑地

④ pat [pæt] *v.* 轻拍
⑤ spring [spriŋ] *n.* 跳跃

　　一天，腓力国王买下了一匹骏马，它的名字叫布西发拉斯。这是一头高贵的牲畜，为了得到它，国王花了很高的价钱。然而，这匹马的脾气非常暴躁，没有人能够驾驭它，大家对它都感到束手无策。

　　人们曾经试图用鞭子来制服它，可这样做只会让马的脾气变得更坏。迫不得已，国王只好让仆人把它牵走。

　　"太可惜了，这么好的一匹骏马就这样给毁了。"国王的小儿子亚历山大说："那些人根本不懂得怎样对待它。"

　　"兴许你能比他们做得更好！"父亲嘲笑地说。

　　"那当然！"亚历山大说，"只要你让我试一试，一定能够让这匹马变得服服帖帖。"

　　"如果你没有做到，那该怎么办？"腓力国王问。

　　"我把买马的钱赔给你。"小伙子说。

　　在众人的哄笑声中，亚历山大跑到布西发拉斯身旁，让马头朝向太阳。他已经观察到，这匹马害怕看见自己的影子。

　　然后亚历山大轻声地对马说着话，用手抚摸着它的身子。等马稍微安静下来，王子迅速一跃，骑到了马背上。

Everybody expected to see the boy killed **outright**①. But he kept his place, and let the horse run as fast as he would. By and by, when Bucephalus had become tired, Alexander reined him in, and rode back to the place where his father was standing.

All the men who were there shouted when they saw that the boy had proved himself to be the master of the horse.

He leaped to the ground, and his father ran and kissed him.

"My son," said the king, "Macedon is too small a place for you. You must seek a larger kingdom that will be worthy of you."

After that, Alexander and Bucephalus were the best of friends. They were said to be always together, for when one of them was seen, the other was sure to be not far away. But the horse would never allow any one to mount him but his master.

Alexander became the most famous king and warrior that was ever known; and for that reason he is always called Alexander the Great. Bucephalus carried him through many countries and in many fierce battles, and more than once did he save his master's life.

所有人都以为这个孩子肯定会当场被摔死。可是王子却稳坐在马背上，骑着马飞快地跑了起来。慢慢地，布西发拉斯跑累了，亚历山大勒住马，把它骑回父亲站的地方。

　　看到这个孩子已经证明他就是马的主人，所有人都欢呼了起来。

　　男孩从马背上跳下来，父亲立刻跑过去亲吻他。

　　"我的儿子，"国王说，"马其顿这个地方对你来说太小了，你应该去找一个更大的王国去发挥你的才能。"

　　从此以后，亚历山大和布西发拉斯成为了最好的朋友。据说他们一直待在一起，形影不离。可是除了主人之外，那匹马不允许任何人碰它。

　　后来，亚历山大成为举世闻名的国王和勇士，人们都称他为亚历山大大帝。布西发拉斯载着国王，足迹踏遍了许多国家，也经历过很多激烈的战斗，而且还不止一次地救过主人的性命。

① outright ['autrait] *ad.* 立刻地

35. Diogenes the Wise Man

At Corinth, in Greece, there lived a very wise man whose name was Diogenes. Men came from all parts of the land to see him and hear him talk.

But wise as he was, he had some very **queer**[①] ways. He did not believe that any man ought to have more things than he really needed; and he said that no man needed much. And so he did not live in a house, but slept in a **tub**[②] or barrel, which he rolled about from place to place. He spent his days sitting in the sun, and saying wise things to those who were around him.

At noon one day, Diogenes was seen walking through the streets with a lighted lantern, and looking all around as if in search of something.

"Why do you carry a lantern when the sun is shining?" some one said.

"I am looking for an honest man," answered Diogenes.

When Alexander the Great went to Corinth, all the foremost men in the city came out to see him and to praise him. But Diogenes did not come; and he was the only man for whose opinions Alexander cared.

And so, since the wise man would not come to see the king, the king went to see the wise man. He found Diogenes in an out-of-the-way place, lying on the ground by his tub. He was enjoying the heat and the light of the sun.

When he saw the king and a great many people coming, he sat up and looked at Alexander. Alexander greeted him and said,—

35. 智者第欧根尼

① queer [kwiə] *a.* 奇怪的

② tub [tʌb] *n.* 桶

希腊的科林斯有一位名叫第欧根尼的智者。为了聆听他的教诲，人们从全国各地赶到这里来见他。

尽管身为智者，第欧根尼却有一些十分古怪的生活方式。他认为人们没必要拥有比实际需要还要多的东西，而且说人们需要的其实并不多。第欧根尼不在房子里面住，却宁愿睡在木桶里，无论走到哪里，木桶就跟着他滚到那里。白天，他会坐在太阳下面，跟围在身边的人们讲他的智慧。

一天中午，人们看见第欧根尼提着一个亮着的灯笼在大街上走，他好像在四处寻找什么东西。

"大白天太阳当空，你提个灯笼干什么？"有人问。

"我在寻找诚实的人。"第欧根尼回答说。

亚历山大大帝来到科林斯，城里所有的体面人都出来迎接他，赞美他。可是第欧根尼没有露面，而亚历山大大帝对他的看法却最在意。

既然这位智者不来见他，国王便前去拜访他。在一个很偏僻的地方，国王找到了第欧根尼，当时他正躺在木桶旁边的地上，惬意地晒着太阳。

看到很多人拥着国王走了过来，第欧根尼坐直了身

Diogenes and Alexander

"Diogenes, I have heard a great deal about your wisdom. Is there anything that I can do for you?"

"Yes," said Diogenes. "You can stand a little on one side, so as not to keep the sunshine from me."

This answer was so different from what he expected, that the king was much surprised. But it did not make him angry; it only made him admire the strange man all the more. When he turned to ride back, he said to his officers,—

"Say what you will; if I were not Alexander, I would like to be Diogenes."

第欧根尼和亚历山大大帝

子望着他。国王先跟他打招呼，说：——

"第欧根尼，你的智慧我早有耳闻，我能为你做些什么吗？"

"能。"第欧根尼回答道，"你能不能稍微往旁边让一让，你挡住了我的阳光。"

这个回答远远超出国王的想象，他感到十分意外，但并没有生气，反而更加佩服眼前的这个怪人。国王骑马返回的时候，对官员们说：

"不管怎么说，如果我不是亚历山大，我宁愿成为第欧根尼。"

36. The Brave Three Hundred

All Greece was in danger. A mighty army, led by the great King of Persia, had come from the east. It was marching along the seashore, and in a few days would be in Greece. The great king had sent messengers into every city and state, bidding them give him water and earth **in token**[①] that the land and the sea were his. But they said, —

"No: we will be free."

And so there was a great **stir**[②] throughout all the land. The men armed themselves, and made haste to go out and drive back their foe; and the women **staid**[③] at home, weeping and waiting, and trembling with fear.

There was only one way by which the Persian army could go into Greece on that side, and that was by a narrow pass between the mountains and the sea. This pass was guarded by Leonidas, the King of the Spartans, with three hundred Spartan soldiers.

Soon the Persian soldiers were seen coming. There were so many of them that no man could count them. How could a handful of men hope to stand against so great a host?

And yet Leonidas and his Spartans held their ground. They had made up their minds to die at their post. Some one brought them word that there were so many Persians that their arrows darkened the sun.

36. 三百名勇士

① in token 作为标志；以表示……

② stir [stəː] n. 轰动

③ staid [steid] v.〔古语〕stay 的过去式和过去分词

波斯国王率领一支强大的军队沿着海岸线从东边打了过来。再过几日，他们就要到达希腊，希腊全国都陷入了危机之中。这位国王派使者给全国各地传话，让他们献上那里的水和土，以此来表示这些领地和领海都臣服于他，可是这些地方的人却说：

"不，我们要自由！"

于是，希腊全国陷入了动荡。男人们把自己武装起来，匆匆忙忙出去驱赶敌人；女人们则留在家里哭泣等待，惊恐不安。

波斯军队要进入希腊只有一条路可走。那是一条位于群山和大海之间的狭窄通道，斯巴达国王李奥尼达斯率领三百名斯巴达士兵正驻守在那里。

很快，波斯军队进入了斯巴达人的视线，他们人多势众，斯巴达人仅凭这么一小队人马，怎么能够抵挡得住如此强大的军队啊？

然而，李奥尼达斯和他的斯巴达士兵们依然坚守在阵地上，决心要与阵地共存亡。有人传来消息说，波斯人实在太多了，射出去的箭都能够遮住太阳。

"So much the better," said the Spartans; "we shall fight in the shade."

Bravely they stood in the narrow pass. Bravely they faced their foes. To Spartans there was no such thing as fear. The Persians came forward, only to meet death at the points of their spears.

But one by one the Spartans fell. At last their spears were broken; yet still they stood side by side, fighting to the last. Some fought with swords, some with **daggers**①, and some with only their fists and teeth.

All day long the army of the Persians was kept at bay. But when the sun went down, there was not one Spartan left alive. Where they had stood there was only a heap of the slain, all **bristled**② over with spears and arrows.

Twenty thousand Persian soldiers had fallen before that handful of men. And Greece was saved.

Thousands of years have passed since then; but men still like to tell the story of Leonidas and the brave three hundred who died for their country's sake.

"这样更好！"斯巴达人说，"如果真是那样，那我们就能在阴凉里战斗了。"

斯巴达人站在狭窄的关口上，英勇地痛击着来犯之敌，心里毫不畏惧。如果波斯人胆敢冲过来，就让他们死在长矛之下。

斯巴达人一个接一个地倒下了，最后他们的长矛也折断了，可依然一起并肩作战。他们用剑和匕首，还有拳头和牙齿，一直浴血奋战到最后一刻。

整整一天，波斯军队寸步难进。太阳落山时分，斯巴达人全部壮烈牺牲，他们战斗过的地方只留下一堆堆的尸体，上面插满了长矛和弓箭。

然而，两万名波斯士兵却倒在了这一小队斯巴达人面前，希腊得救了。

数千年过去了，人们依然喜欢谈论李奥尼达斯和三百名勇士为国捐躯的故事。

① dagger ['dægə] *n.* 匕首

② bristle ['brisl] *v.* （密密地）覆盖

37. Socrates and His House

There once lived in Greece a very wise man whose name was Socrates. Young men from all parts of the land went to him to learn wisdom from him; and he said so many pleasant things, and said them in so delightful a way, that no one ever grew tired of listening to him.

One summer he built himself a house, but it was so small that his neighbors wondered how he could be content with it.

"What is the reason," said they, "that you, who are so great a man, should build such a little box as this for your dwelling house?"

"Indeed, there may be little reason," said he; "but, small as the place is, I shall think myself happy if I can fill even it with true friends."

37. 苏格拉底和他的房子

　　从前，希腊有一个富有智慧的哲人名叫苏格拉底，年轻人从全国各地赶来向他学习智慧，苏格拉底给他们讲了很多有趣的事情。由于讲的方式轻松愉快，听众们从来不会感到厌倦。

　　有一年夏天，苏格拉底给自己修建了一座很小的房子，邻居们都很奇怪他怎么会满足于这样一座房子。

　　"为什么像你这样伟大的人，"邻居们问，"却要修一座像小盒子一样大的房子住？"

　　"的确，这种做法看起来似乎很不合情理。"苏格拉底说，"这个房子是小了点，可是如果它的里面能够装满真正的朋友，那我也就心满意足了。"

38. The King and His Hawk

Genghis Khan was a great king and warrior.

He led his army into China and Persia, and he conquered many lands. In every country, men told about his daring deeds; and they said that since Alexander the Great there had been no king like him.

One morning when he was home from the wars, he rode out into the woods to have a day's sport. Many of his friends were with him. They rode out **gaily**[①], carrying their bows and arrows. Behind them came the servants with the hounds.

It was a **merry**[②] hunting party. The woods rang with their shouts and laughter. They expected to carry much **game**[③] home in the evening.

On the king's wrist sat his favorite hawk; for in those days hawks were trained to hunt. At a word from their masters they would fly high up into the air, and look around for **prey**[④]. If they chanced to see a deer or a rabbit, they would swoop down upon it swift as any arrow.

All day long Genghis Khan and his huntsmen rode through the woods. But they did not find as much game as they expected.

Toward evening they started for home. The king had often ridden through the woods, and he knew all the paths. So while the rest of the party took the nearest

38. 国王和鹰

① gaily ['geili] ad. 欢乐地

② merry ['meri] a. 愉快的

③ game [geim] n. 猎物

④ prey [prei] n. 被捕的动物

成吉思汗曾经是一位伟大的国王和勇士。

这位国王带领军队占领了中国和波斯，还让很多国家俯首称臣，全世界的人都在传颂他的英勇事迹。人们说自从亚历山大大帝以后，还没有哪位国王能够和成吉思汗相提并论。

一天早晨，成吉思汗从战场上回来，准备骑马去森林里打一天猎，同行的还有很多朋友。他们骑着马，带着弓箭，身后跟着仆人和猎狗，高高兴兴地出发了。

这次狩猎真的是一次快乐的聚会，森林里回荡着成吉思汗和朋友们的欢声笑语，大家盼望晚上回去的时候能够多打些猎物。

国王最钟爱的猎鹰停在他的手腕上。当时的人们训练老鹰捕猎，主人只要发出命令，老鹰就会飞向高空寻找周围的猎物。如果刚好看到一只鹿或一只野兔，老鹰就会快速扑下去抓住猎物，其速度不输弓箭。

成吉思汗和同伴们在森林里骑马走了整整一天，可是并没有找到他们希望的那么多猎物。

傍晚时分，他们准备回家。国王以前经常到这片林子里来，对这里的每一条道路都谙熟于心。别的同伴都

· 195 ·

Fifty Famous Stories Retold

way, he went by a longer road through a valley between two mountains.

The day had been warm, and the king was very thirsty. His pet hawk had left his wrist and flown away. It would be sure to find its way home.

The king rode slowly along. He had once seen a **spring**① of clear water near this pathway. If he could only find it now! But the hot days of summer had dried up all the mountain **brooks**②.

At last, to his joy, he saw some water trickling down over the edge of a rock. He knew that there was a spring farther up. In the wet season, a swift stream of water always poured down here; but now it came only one drop at a time.

The king leaped from his horse. He took a little silver cup from his hunting bag. He held it so as to catch the slowly falling drops.

It took a long time to fill the cup; and the king was so thirsty that he could hardly wait. At last it was nearly full. He put the cup to his lips, and was about to drink.

All at once there was a **whirring**③ sound in the air, and the cup was knocked from his hands. The water was all **spilled**④ upon the ground.

The king looked up to see who had done this thing. It was his pet hawk.

The hawk flew back and forth a few times, and then alighted among the rocks by the spring.

The king picked up the cup, and again held it to catch the trickling drops.

This time he did not wait so long. When the cup was half full, he lifted it toward his mouth. But before it had touched his lips, the hawk swooped down again, and knocked it from his hands.

And now the king began to grow angry. He tried again; and for the third time the hawk kept him from drinking.

The king was now very angry indeed.

"How do you dare to act so?" he cried. "If I had you in my hands, I would

① spring [sprɪŋ] *n.* 泉水

② brook [brʊk] *n.* 小溪

③ whir [hwəː] *v.* 作呼呼声
④ spill [spɪl] *v.* 使溢出

抄近道回去了，只有国王独自一人走上了一条稍远一点的路，它位于两座大山之间的山谷里。

天气很热，国王觉得口渴难耐。他的猎鹰已经不见了踪影，肯定是出去寻找回家的路了。

国王沿着道路慢慢骑着。以前，他曾经在路旁看见过一股清澈的泉水，要是现在能找到它该多好啊！可不巧的是，现在正值炎炎夏日，山上的小溪都干涸了。

让国王感到高兴的是，他看见山上一块岩石的边上正在滴水。他知道山上更远的地方有泉水，每逢雨季，这里总有一股湍急的水流倾泻而下，可是现在只剩下断断续续流下的水滴了。

国王跳下马，从狩猎袋里取出小银杯，准备去接那些徐徐落下来的水滴。

可是要把杯子接满需要很长的时间。国王实在口渴难耐，几乎等不及了，还没等杯子接满，就急着去喝杯子里的水。

突然，空中响起了一阵呼呼急飞的声音，紧接着国王手中的杯子被打掉了，里面的水也全部倒掉了。

国王抬起头，想看看是谁打翻了他的杯子，原来是他的爱鹰。

那只鹰在空中来来回回飞了几次，然后停在泉水旁边的岩石上。

国王捡起杯子，又准备去接水。

这一次杯子刚接到半满，国王就想去喝。可还没等杯子到他的嘴边，那只鹰又一次俯冲下来，把他手中的杯子撞掉。

国王的火气蹭地一下上来了。他又去接了一次水，鹰又第三次阻止了他。

国王现在真的发脾气了。

"你好大的胆子！"他大喊道，"如果你在我的手上，

wring① your neck!"

Then he filled the cup again. But before he tried to drink, he drew his sword.

"Now, Sir Hawk," he said, "this is the last time."

He had hardly spoken, before the hawk swooped down and knocked the cup from his hand. But the king was looking for this. With a quick **sweep**② of the sword he struck the bird as it passed.

The next moment the poor hawk lay bleeding and dying at its master's feet.

"That is what you get for your pains," said Genghis Khan.

But when he looked for his cup, he found that it had fallen between two rocks, where he could not reach it.

"At any rate, I will have a drink from that spring," he said to himself.

With that he began to climb the steep bank to the place from which the water trickled. It was hard work, and the higher he climbed, the thirstier he became.

At last he reached the place. There indeed was a pool of water; but what was that lying in the pool, and almost filling it? It was a huge, dead snake of the most poisonous kind.

① wring [riŋ] *v.* 拧

② sweep [swi:p] *n.* 挥动

我一定会扭断你的脖子!"

话音刚落,国王又准备去接水。这一次在喝水之前,他顺便拔出了宝剑。

"现在,老鹰先生,"国王说,"这是最后一次了。"

国王的话音刚落,鹰又一次冲下来把他手中的杯子打翻。国王瞅准了时机,趁老鹰飞过的时候,拿起宝剑飞快地一击。

可怜的老鹰淌着血,奄奄一息地躺在主人的脚下。

"这是你咎由自取!"成吉思汗说。

再去找杯子时,国王发现它掉进了两块岩石中间一个够不到的地方。

"不管怎么样,我都要喝水。"国王自言自语道。

于是,国王沿着陡峭的山坡向那个滴水的地方爬去;山路实在太难走了,爬得越高,他就觉得越渴。

国王终于爬到了那个地方,看见那里的确有一个水潭,可是里面好像躺着一个什么东西。天啊,原来是一条剧毒的死蛇,它的巨大身躯几乎填满了整个水潭。

The king stopped. He forgot his thirst. He thought only of the poor dead bird lying on the ground below him.

"The hawk saved my life!" he cried; "and how did I repay him? He was my best friend, and I have killed him."

He clambered down the bank. He took the bird up gently, and laid it in his hunting bag. Then he mounted his horse and rode swiftly home. He said to himself, —

"I have learned a sad lesson today; and that is, never to do anything in anger."

国王停下脚步，忘记了口渴，心里只有那只躺在下面的老鹰，然而让人惋惜的是它已经死了。

"老鹰救了我的命啊！"国王大叫了起来，"我却恩将仇报。它是我最好的朋友，我却亲手杀了它。"

成吉思汗从山坡上爬下来，把老鹰轻轻捧起来放进狩猎袋里，骑着马，飞快向家里奔去。他一边走一边自言自语道：

"我今天得到了一个惨痛的教训：人在愤怒的时候，千万不能草率行事。"

39. Doctor Goldsmith

There was once a kind man whose name was Oliver Goldsmith. He wrote many delightful books, some of which you will read when you are older.

He had a gentle heart. He was always ready to help others and to share with them anything that he had. He gave away so much to the poor that he was always poor himself.

He was sometimes called Doctor Goldsmith; for he had studied to be a **physician**[①].

One day a poor woman asked Doctor Goldsmith to go and see her husband, who was sick and could not eat.

Goldsmith did so. He found that the family was in great need. The man had not had work for a long time. He was not sick, but in distress; and, as for eating, there was no food in the house.

"Call at my room this evening," said Goldsmith to the woman, "and I will give you some medicine for your husband."

In the evening the woman called. Goldsmith gave her a little paper box that was very heavy.

"Here is the medicine," he said. "Use it faithfully, and I think it will do your

39. 戈德史密斯医生

从前，有一个心地善良的人名叫奥利弗·戈德史密斯。这个人写过许许多多有趣的书籍，有些书你们长大后可能会读到。

戈德史密斯有一颗善良、乐于助人的心，愿意与他人分享自己的一切。他对穷人慷慨赠予，以至于自己总是一贫如洗。

戈德史密斯以前当过医生，所以有时候人们也称他戈德史密斯医生。

一天，一个穷苦的女人来请戈德史密斯医生给她丈夫看病。她丈夫因为生病，吃不下去东西。

戈德史密斯到那里后，发现这家人的生活十分窘迫。实际上男主人没有病，只是因为很久没有出去工作，心里感到忧愁罢了。至于饮食，家里实在找不出什么可以吃的东西了。

"今晚你到我家来。"戈德史密斯对那个女人说："我给你丈夫开些药。"

女人当天晚上来了，戈德史密斯交给她一个沉甸甸的小纸盒。

"药在盒子里面。"戈德史密斯说，"让你丈夫好好

① physician [fi'ziʃən] n. 医生

husband a great deal of good. But don't open the box until you reach home."

"What are the directions for taking it?" asked the woman.

"You will find them inside of the box," he answered.

When the woman reached her home, she sat down by her husband's side, and they opened the box; What do you think they found in it?

It was full of pieces of money. And on the top were the directions:—

"TO BE TAKEN AS OFTEN AS NECESSITY REQUIRES."

Goldsmith had given them all the ready money that he had.

服药，我想这些药对他是有很大好处的；记得到家之前，不要把盒子打开。"

"这些药怎么服用？"女人问。

"服药的说明在盒子里面。"戈德史密斯回答说。

到家后，女人坐在丈夫的身旁把盒子打开。你猜猜看，他们在盒子里发现了什么？

原来盒子里面装满了一块一块的钱币，上面还附着一张说明：

"必要时再用！"

原来，戈德史密斯把自己身上所有的钱都拿出来送给了这家人。

40. The Kingdoms

There was once a king of Prussia whose name was Frederick William.

On a fine morning in June he went out alone to walk in the green woods. He was tired of the noise of the city, and he was glad to get away from it.

So, as he walked among the trees, he often stopped to listen to the singing birds, or to look at the wild flowers that grew on every side. Now and then he **stooped**① to **pluck**② a **violet**③, or a **primrose**④, or a yellow **buttercup**⑤. Soon his hands were full of pretty blossoms.

After a while he came to a little **meadow**⑥ in the midst of the wood. Some children were playing there. They were running here and there, and gathering the **cowslips**⑦ that were blooming among the grass.

It made the king glad to see the happy children, and hear their merry voices. He stood still for some time, and watched them as they played.

Then he called them around him, and all sat down together in the pleasant shade. The children did not know who the strange gentleman was; but they liked his kind face and gentle manners.

"Now, my little folks," said the king, "I want to ask you some questions, and the child who gives the best answer shall have a prize."

Then he held up an orange so that all the children could see.

40. 王国

从前有一个普鲁士国王，名叫腓特烈·威廉。

六月一个晴朗的早晨，国王独自一人来到绿色的树林里，他厌倦城市生活的嘈杂，庆幸自己终于摆脱了出来。

国王行走在林间，时而停下脚步聆听小鸟的歌声，时而看看两边盛开的野花，时而俯下身去摘紫罗兰、樱草花和黄色的金凤花。很快，他的双手就捧满了美丽的花朵。

过了一会儿，国王来到林中的一块小草地上，看见几个小孩正在那里玩耍。他们在草地上跑来跑去，采着盛开的流星花。

国王欣喜地望着那些快乐的孩子，听着他们的欢声笑语，静静地站在那里看着他们玩耍。

然后国王把孩子们叫到身旁，让他们坐在凉爽的树荫下面。孩子们并不知道眼前的这个陌生绅士是谁，但是他们喜欢他和蔼的脸庞和优雅的举止。

"我的小朋友们，"国王说，"现在我要问你们一些问题。谁回答得最好，我就奖给谁一个礼物。"

说完，国王举起一只柳橙，让所有孩子都能够看见它。

① stoop [stu:p] v. 弯腰，俯身
② pluck [plʌk] v. 采摘
③ violet ['vaiələt] n. 紫罗兰花
④ primrose ['primrəuz] n. 樱草花
⑤ buttercup ['bʌtəkʌp] n. 金凤花
⑥ meadow ['medəu] n. 草地
⑦ cowslip ['kau͵slip] n. 流星花

"You know that we all live in the kingdom of Prussia," he said; "but tell me, to what kingdom does this orange belong?"

The children were puzzled. They looked at one another, and sat very still for a little while. Then a brave, bright boy spoke up and said,—

"It belongs to the vegetable kingdom, sir."

"Why so, my lad?" asked the king.

"It is the fruit of a plant, and all plants belong to that kingdom," said the boy.

The king was pleased. "You are quite right," he said; "and you shall have the orange for your prize."

He **tossed**① it gaily to the boy. "Catch it if you can!" he said.

Then he took a yellow gold piece from his pocket, and held it up so that it glittered in the sunlight.

"Now to what kingdom does this belong?" he asked.

Another bright boy answered quickly, "To the mineral kingdom, sir! All metals belong to that kingdom."

"你们知道，我们都生活在普鲁士王国里。"国王说，"可是谁能告诉我，这颗柳橙属于哪一个王国呢？"

孩子们疑惑地你看看我，我看看你，坐在那里沉默了片刻。然后，一个聪明勇敢的男孩大胆地说：

"先生，它属于植物王国。"

"为什么呢，我的孩子？"国王问。

"它是一种植物的果实，所有植物都属于植物王国。"男孩回答说。

国王高兴极了。"你说得很对！"他说，"这个柳橙就作为给你的奖励。"

说完，他高兴地把柳橙抛向男孩。"接住！"国王说。

然后国王又从口袋里拿出一块黄色的金币，高高地举在手上，金币在阳光的照射下闪闪发光。

"现在谁能告诉我，这个属于什么王国呢？"国王又问。

另一个聪明的男孩立刻回答说，"属于矿物王国，

① toss [tɔs] v. 投掷

· 209 ·

"That is a good answer," said the king. "The gold piece is your prize."

The children were delighted. With eager faces they waited to hear what the stranger would say next.

"I will ask you only one more question," said the king, "and it is an easy one." Then he stood up, and said, "Tell me, my little folks, to what kingdom do I belong?"

The bright boys were puzzled now. Some thought of saying, "To the kingdom of Prussia." Some wanted to say, "To the animal kingdom." But they were a little afraid, and all kept still.

At last a tiny blue-eyed child looked up into the king's smiling face, and said in her simple way,—

"I think to the kingdom of heaven."

King Frederick William stooped down and lifted the little maiden in his arms. Tears were in his eyes as he kissed her, and said, "So be it, my child! So be it."

先生！所有的金属都属于矿物王国。"

"回答得对极了！"国王说，"这个金币就是给你的奖励。"

孩子们十分激动，脸上都流露出渴望的神情，他们迫不及待地想听这个陌生人接下来还会问什么。

"我再问你们最后一个问题，"国王说，"这个问题很简单。"说完他站了起来，问："谁能告诉我，我的小朋友们，我属于哪个王国呢？"

那些聪明的孩子们又一次呆住了。有人想说："属于普鲁士王国。"有人想说："属于动物王国。"可是他们都不敢那样讲，大家保持着沉默。

最后，一个长着蓝色眼睛的小不点抬头望着国王微笑的脸庞，天真无邪地说：

"我想你属于天国。"

腓特烈·威廉国王弯腰把小女孩抱了起来，眼中含着泪水亲吻着她，说："就是这样，我的孩子！就是这样。"

41. The Barmecide Feast

There was once a rich old man who was called the Barmecide. He lived in a beautiful palace in the midst of flowery gardens. He had everything that heart could wish.

In the same land there was a poor man whose name was Schacabac. His clothing was rags, and his food was the **scraps**[1] which other people had thrown away. But he had a light heart, and was as happy as a king.

Once when Schacabac had not had anything to eat for a long time, he thought that he would go and ask the Barmecide to help him.

The servant at the door said, "Come in and talk with our master. He will not send you away hungry."

Schacabac went in, and passed through many beautiful rooms, looking for the Barmecide. At last he came to a grand hall where there were soft carpets on the floor, and fine pictures on the walls, and pleasant **couches**[2] to lie down upon.

At the upper end of the room he saw a noble man with a long white beard. It was the Barmecide; and poor Schacabac bowed low before him, as was the custom in that country.

The Barmecide spoke very kindly, and asked what was wanted.

41. 巴米赛德的盛宴

　　从前，有一个老富翁名叫巴米赛德。此人住在百花盛开的花园中一座美丽的宫殿里面，拥有人们渴望的一切财富。

　　在同一个地区，住着一个名叫沙加巴克的穷人，他衣衫褴褛，吃着别人扔掉的残羹剩饭。可是沙加巴克有一颗快乐的心，快乐得就像国王一样。

　　一次，沙加巴克已经很久没有吃到东西了，便去巴米赛德那里希望得到帮助。

　　门口的仆人说："进来和我们的主人说说吧！他是不会让你饿着肚子离开的。"

　　沙加巴克走进去寻找巴米赛德，一路上穿过了很多漂亮的房间，最后来到一个华丽的大厅里面。大厅的地上铺着柔软的地毯，墙上挂着精美的图画，里面还摆放着舒适的沙发供人们躺下休息。

　　在大厅的尽头，沙加巴克看到一个高贵的人，此人留着长长的白胡须，他就是巴米赛德。穷人沙加巴克按照这个国家的礼节深鞠一躬向巴米赛德行礼。

　　巴米赛德说起话来十分和蔼，问沙加巴克需要什么帮助。

① scrap [skræp] *n.* 残余物

② couch [kautʃ] *n.* 长沙发

Schacabac told him about all his troubles, and said that it was now two days since he had tasted bread.

"Is it possible?" said the Barmecide. "You must be almost dead with hunger; and here I have plenty and to **spare**①!"

Then he turned and called, "Ho, boy! Bring in the water to wash our hands, and then order the cook to hurry the supper."

Schacabac had not expected to be treated so kindly. He began to thank the rich man.

"Say not a word," said the Barmecide, "but let us get ready for the **feast**②."

Then the rich man began to rub his hands as though some one was pouring water on them. "Come and wash with me," he said.

Schacabac saw no boy, nor **basin**③, nor water. But he thought that he ought to do as he was bidden; and so, like the Barmecide, he made a pretense of washing.

"Come now," said the Barmecide, "let us have supper."

He sat down, as if to a table, and pretended to be carving a **roast**④. Then he said, "Help yourself, my good friend. You said you were hungry: so, now, don't be afraid of the food."

Schacabac thought that he understood the joke, and he made pretense of taking food, and passing it to his mouth. Then he began to chew, and said, "You see, sir, I **lose no time**⑤."

"Boy," said the old man, "bring on the roast goose.—Now, my good friend, try this choice piece from the breast. And here are sweet sauce, honey, **raisins**⑥, green peas, and dry **figs**⑦. Help yourself, and remember that other good things are coming."

Schacabac was almost dead with hunger, but he was too polite not to do as he was bidden.

"Come," said the Barmecide, "have another piece of the roast lamb. Did you ever eat anything so delicious?"

① spare [spɛə] *v.* 供给，匀出

② feast [fi:st] *n.* 丰盛的饭菜

③ basin ['beisən] *n.* 盆

④ roast [rəust] *n.* 烤肉

⑤ lose no time 立即行动

⑥ raisin ['reizən] *n.* 葡萄干
⑦ fig [fig] *n.* 无花果

沙加巴克把自己的困难都告诉了他，还说自己已经两天没有吃到面包了。

"真的吗？"巴米赛德说，"那你一定快要饿死了。我这里有很多东西，你可以随便吃！"

说完，巴米赛德转过身喊道："嗨，仆人！拿些水过来让我们洗手，再吩咐厨师快点准备晚餐。"

沙加巴克没有想到竟然会得到这样的礼遇，便向巴米赛德连声道谢。

"你什么话都不用说。"巴米赛德说，"现在让我们准备饱餐一顿！"

说完，这个富人开始搓着双手，就好像有人正在往他手上倒水一样。"过来和我一起洗吧！"巴米赛德招呼着。

沙加巴克没有看到仆人，也没有看到水盆，更没有看到水。可是他想，最好还是按照吩咐的去做，于是便模仿起巴米赛德的样子，假装洗起手来。

"来吧！"巴米赛德又说，"现在我们开始吃晚餐吧！"

巴米赛德坐了下去，就好像坐在一张桌子的旁边，假装正在切烤肉。接着他又说："请随便用，我的好朋友。你说你饿坏了，现在干吗不吃呢。"

沙加巴克心想，这不就是闹着玩的嘛！于是，他假装拿起食物放进嘴里嚼了起来，并且说："你看，先生，我都等不及了。"

"仆人，"巴米赛德吩咐道，"去把烤鹅端上来。我的好朋友，现在品尝一下胸部最好的这块肉。这里还有甜酱、蜂蜜、葡萄干、绿豆和无花果干，请随便用，其他佳肴也马上端上来了。"

沙加巴克几乎快饿死了，可是他依然不失礼节，按照吩咐的去做。

"来吧！"巴米赛德说，"再来一块烤羊肉。你吃没吃过这么美味的东西？"

· 215 ·

"Never in my life," said Schacabac. "Your table is full of good things."

"Then eat heartily," said the Barmecide. "You cannot please me better."

After this came the dessert. The Barmecide spoke of sweetmeats and fruits; and Schacabac made believe that he was eating them.

"Now is there anything else that you would like?" asked the host.

"Ah, no!" said poor Schacabac. "I have indeed had great plenty."

"Let us drink, then," said the Barmecide. "Boy, bring on the wine!"

"Excuse me, my lord," said Schacabac, "I will drink no wine, for it is forbidden."

The Barmecide seized him by the hand. "I have long wished to find a man like you," he said. "But come, now we will **sup**[1] in earnest."

He clapped his hands. Servants came, and he ordered supper. Soon they sat down to a table loaded with the very dishes of which they had pretended to eat.

Poor Schacabac had never had so good a meal in all his life. When they had finished, and the table had been cleared away, the Barmecide said,—

"I have found you to be a man of good understanding. Your wits are quick, and you are ready always to make the best of everything. Come and live with me, and manage my house."

And so Schacabac lived with the Barmecide many years, and never again knew what it was to be hungry.

"从来没有。"沙加巴克说,"桌上的东西好丰盛啊!"

"那就尽情吃吧!"巴米赛德说,"没有什么能更令我高兴的了。"

甜点上来了。巴米赛德提到甜食和水果,沙加巴克也假装吃到了。

"现在你还需要别的什么东西吗?"巴米赛德问。

"啊,不!"可怜的沙加巴克说,"我真的已经吃不下了。"

"那我们喝点酒吧!"巴米赛德说,"仆人,把酒端上来。"

"对不起,老爷。"沙加巴克说,"我不喝酒,酒是禁止喝的。"

巴米赛德一把抓住沙加巴克的手。"我一直在找一个像你这样的人,已经找了很久了。"他说。"快来,现在我们去吃真正的晚餐。"

说完,巴米赛德拍了拍手。仆人们进来了,巴米赛德安排好了晚餐。很快,他们坐在桌旁,桌子上面摆满了那些他们刚才假装吃过的菜肴。

可怜的沙加巴克一辈子也没有吃过这么丰盛的饭菜。吃完饭桌子收拾停当,巴米赛德说:

"我发现你是一个十分善解人意的人。你的头脑敏捷,随时准备把每件事情做到最好。搬来和我一起住吧,我想让你做我的管家。"

于是,沙加巴克和巴米赛德在一起生活了很多年。从此以后,沙加巴克再也不知道什么是饥饿了。

① sup [sʌp] v. 吃晚饭

42. The Endless Tale

In the Far East there was a great king who had no work to do. Every day, and all day long, he sat on soft cushions and listened to stories. And no matter what the story was about, he never grew tired of hearing it, even though it was very long.

"There is only one fault that I find with your story," he often said: "it is too short."

All the storytellers in the world were invited to his palace; and some of them told tales that were very long indeed. But the king was always sad when a story was ended.

At last he sent word into every city and town and country place, offering a prize to any one who should tell him an endless tale. He said,—

"To the man that will tell me a story which shall last forever, I will give my fairest daughter for his wife; and I will make him my heir, and he shall be king after me."

But this was not all. He added a very hard condition. "If any man shall try to tell such a story and then fail, he shall have his head cut off."

The king's daughter was very pretty, and there were many young men in that country who were willing to do anything to win her. But none of them wanted to lose their heads, and so only a few tried for the prize.

42. 讲不完的故事

遥远的东方有一个大国的国王。此人整天无所事事，喜欢坐在一张柔软的垫子上听人讲故事。不管什么样的故事，即便再长，他都不会感到厌烦。

国王常说："我觉得你的故事只有一个缺点，就是太短了。"

凡是世界上会讲故事的人都会被请到王宫里面。有些人讲的故事的确很长，可是每次故事一结束，国王就会感到难过。

最后国王派人传话给全国各地，悬赏寻找一位能讲一个永远也不会结束的故事的人。他说：

"如果谁能给我讲一个永远也讲不完的故事，我就要把我最漂亮的女儿嫁给他，并且让他继承我的王位。"

当然，这还不是全部，国王又附加了一个十分苛刻的条件："如果这个人没能把故事一直讲下去，那他就要人头落地。"

国王的女儿非常漂亮，为赢得她的芳心，那个国家的很多年轻人愿意去做任何事情。当然，人们谁也不愿意丢掉自己的脑袋，所以愿意为了这个奖赏去冒险的人寥寥无几。

· 219 ·

Fifty Famous Stories Retold

One young man invented a story that lasted three months; but at the end of that time, he could think of nothing more. His fate was a warning to others, and it was a long time before another storyteller was so rash as to try the king's patience.

But one day a stranger from the South came into the palace.

"Great king," he said, "is it true that you offer a prize to the man who can tell a story that has no end?"

"It is true," said the king.

"And shall this man have your fairest daughter for his wife, and shall he be your heir?"

"Yes, if he succeeds," said the king. "But if he fails, he shall lose his head."

"Very well, then," said the stranger. "I have a pleasant story about **locusts**① which I would like to relate."

"Tell it," said the king. "I will listen to you."

The storyteller began his tale.

"Once upon a time a certain king seized upon all the corn in his country, and stored it away in a strong **granary**②. But a **swarm**③ of locusts came over the land and saw where the grain had been put. After searching for many days they found on the east side of the granary a crevice that was just large enough for one locust to pass through at a time. So one locust went in and carried away a grain of corn; then another locust went in and carried away a grain of corn; then another locust went in and carried away a grain of corn."

Day after day, week after week, the man kept on saying, "Then another locust went in and carried away a grain of corn."

A month passed; a year passed. At the end of two years, the king said,—

"How much longer will the locusts be going in and carrying away corn?"

"O king!" said the storyteller, "they have as yet cleared only one **cubit**④; and there are many thousand cubits in the granary."

· 220 ·

一次，有个年轻人编了一个能讲三个月的故事，可是到三个月结束的时候，他什么也讲不出来了，他的命运对其他的人也是个警示。因此这件事过去了很久之后，才有人斗胆去讲故事来考验国王的耐心。

这天，有一个从南方来的外乡人走进了王宫。

"大王，"此人说道，"听说如果有人能够讲一个永远讲不完的故事，您就会奖赏他，这是真的吗？"

"是真的。"国王回答道。

"这个人能娶到您最美丽的女儿做妻子，还会成为您的继承人？"

"是的，如果他能够成功的话。"国王说，"可是他如果失败了，那就要掉脑袋。"

"那太好了。"陌生人说，"我想讲一个有关蝗虫的有趣故事。"

"讲吧！"国王说，"我洗耳恭听。"

于是，这个人开始了他的故事：

"从前，有一个国王敛取了国家所有的谷子，把它们装在一个坚固的谷仓里面。一大群蝗虫来到这里，发现了粮食存放的地方。经过很多天的搜寻，它们发现谷仓的东边有一个小缝隙，大小刚好每次让一只蝗虫通过。于是，一只蝗虫进去搬出了一粒谷子，然后另一只蝗虫进去又搬出一粒谷子，然后另一只蝗虫进去又搬出了一粒谷子。"

就这样，时间一天天地过去了，此人还在继续他的故事："然后另一只蝗虫进去又搬出了一粒谷子。"

一个月过去了，一年过去了。到了第二年年底的时候，国王问：

"还要多长时间那些蝗虫才能把谷子搬完？"

"啊，国王陛下！"讲故事的人说，"蝗虫才搬了一腕尺的谷子，谷仓里还有几千腕尺谷子呢！"

① locust ['ləukəst] *n.* 蝗虫

② granary ['grænəri] *n.* 谷仓

③ swarm [swɔːm] *n.* 一大群

④ cubit ['kjuːbit] *n.* 腕尺（古时的长度单位）

· 221 ·

"Man, man!" cried the king, "you will drive me mad. I can listen to it no longer. Take my daughter; be my heir; rule my kingdom. But do not let me hear another word about those horrible locusts!"

And so the strange storyteller married the king's daughter. And he lived happily in the land for many years. But his father-in-law, the king, did not care to listen to any more stories.

"天啊！天啊！"国王大叫了起来，"我快要被你的故事弄疯了，我再也不想听下去了。赶快把我的女儿娶走，来做我的继承人统治国家吧，只要不让我再听到那些可怕的蝗虫就行！"

于是，这个讲故事的陌生人娶了国王的女儿，在那里快乐地生活了许多年。只是他的岳父——那位国王，从此以后再也不想听到任何故事了。

43. The Blind Men and the Elephant

There were once six blind men who stood by the roadside every day, and begged from the people who passed. They had often heard of elephants, but they had never seen one; for, being blind, how could they?

It so happened one morning that an elephant was driven down the road where they stood. When they were told that the great **beast**[①] was before them, they asked the driver to let him stop so that they might see him.

Of course they could not see him with their eyes; but they thought that by touching him they could learn just what kind of animal he was.

The first one happened to put his hand on the elephant's side. "Well, well!" he said, "now I know all about this beast. He is exactly like a wall."

The second felt only of the elephant's **tusk**[②]. "My brother," he said, "you are mistaken. He is not at all like a wall. He is round and smooth and sharp. He is more like a spear than anything else."

The third happened to take hold of the elephant's **trunk**[③]. "Both of you are wrong," he said. "Anybody who knows anything can see that this elephant is like a snake."

The fourth reached out his arms, and grasped one of the elephant's legs. "Oh,

43. 盲人摸象

从前有六个盲人，每天站在路旁向路人乞讨。他们常听人们说起大象，可是自己却从来没有见过大象。他们是盲人，又怎么能够看见大象呢？

一天早晨，正好有人赶着一只大象从那条路上经过。听说巨兽就在面前，盲人们让赶象的人停下来，好让他们看一看大象的模样。

当然，他们无法用眼睛去看大象，但是他们觉得只要用手去摸摸大象，就可以知道大象究竟是什么样的动物了。

第一个盲人走过去后，刚好把手放在大象身体的一侧。"好！好！"他说，"现在我知道大象长什么样了，它长得像一堵墙。"

第二个盲人过去只摸到了象牙。"我的兄弟，"他说，"你说得不对，它根本不像一堵墙。它是圆的，既光滑又尖锐，再没有什么东西比它更像一支长矛了。"

第三个盲人碰巧抓住了大象的鼻子。"你们两个说得都不对！"他说，"凡是稍有常识的人，都能够看出大象长得像一条蛇。"

第四个人伸出双臂抱住大象的一条腿。"啊，你们

---

① beast [bi:st] *n.* 野兽

② tusk [tʌsk] *n.* 长牙

③ trunk [trʌŋk] *n.* 象鼻

how blind you are!" he said. "It is very plain to me that he is round and tall like a tree."

The fifth was a very tall man, and he chanced to take hold of the elephant's ear. "The blindest man ought to know that this beast is not like any of the things that you name," he said. "He is exactly like a huge fan."

The sixth was very blind indeed, and it was some time before he could find the elephant at all. At last he seized the animal's tail. "O foolish fellows!" he cried. "You surely have lost your senses. This elephant is not like a wall, or a spear, or a snake, or a tree; neither is he like a fan. But any man with a **particle**[①] of sense can see that he is exactly like a rope."

Then the elephant moved on, and the six blind men sat by the roadside all day, and quarreled about him. Each believed that he knew just how the animal looked; and each called the others hard names because they did not agree with him. People who have eyes sometimes act as foolishly.

的眼睛真是太瞎了！"他说，"对我来说再明白不过了。大象长得又高又圆，像一棵大树。"

第五个盲人是个高个子，正好抓住了大象的一只耳朵。"连眼睛最瞎的人都应该知道，这个动物长得不像你们提到过的任何东西。"他说，"它长得像一把大扇子。"

第六个盲人眼睛真的很瞎，花了好一会儿工夫才找到大象，最后他抓住了大象的尾巴。"啊，你们这些愚蠢的家伙！"他叫道，"你们一定失去了判断力。这头大象根本不像墙，也不像长矛、蛇或者树，更不像一把扇子。但凡有一丁点判断力的人都能够看出，大象其实长得像一根绳子。"

最后大象被带走了，六个盲人坐在路边争论了一整天。每个人都坚持只有自己才知道大象的模样；他们不同意其他人的说法，相互咒骂指责。即使眼睛明亮的人，有时也会做出类似盲人摸象的愚蠢行为。

① particle ['pɑːtikl] *n.* 微量

Fifty Famous Stories Retold

44. Maximilian and the Goose Boy

One summer day King Maximilian of Bavaria was walking in the country. The sun shone hot, and he stopped under a tree to rest.

It was very pleasant in the cool shade. The king lay down on the soft grass, and looked up at the white clouds sailing across the sky. Then he took a little book from his pocket and tried to read.

But the king could not keep his mind on his book. Soon his eyes closed, and he was fast asleep.

It was past noon when he awoke. He got up from his grassy bed, and looked around. Then he took his **cane**[1] in his hand, and started for home.

When he had walked a mile or more, he happened to think of his book. He felt for it in his pocket. It was not there. He had left it under the tree.

The king was already quite tired, and he did not like to walk back so far. But he did not wish to lose the book. What should he do? If there was only some one to **send for**[2] it!

While he was thinking, he happened to see a little **barefooted**[3] boy in the open field near the road. He was tending a large flock of geese that were picking the short grass, and wading in a shallow brook.

44. 麦克西米利安和放鹅的小孩

有一年盛夏，巴伐利亚国王麦克西米利安在乡间散步。骄阳似火，天气炎热，国王停下脚步，来到一棵树下休息。

凉爽的树荫下面惬意极了。国王躺在柔软的草地上，仰望着天空中飘来飘去的白云，然后从口袋里拿出一本小书看着。

不过国王很难把注意力集中到书上面。不大一会儿工夫，他闭上了眼睛睡着了。

等国王一觉醒来，时间已经过了中午时分。他从那草地上站了起来，向四周望了望，然后拿起手杖准备回家。

国王走了一英里多路的时候，忽然想起了他的书。他摸了一下口袋，发现书已经不见了。原来，他把书忘在了刚才歇息的那棵树下面。

当时国王已经觉得十分疲惫，不想再折回去走那么远的路，可他又不想失去那本书。那该怎么办？如果能派人去把书取回来该多好啊！

就在国王这么想的时候，他看见路边的旷野里站着一个赤脚的小男孩。那个孩子正看管着一大群在浅水中吃草的鹅。

① cane [kein] *n.* 手杖

② send for 派人去叫某人 / 取某物
③ barefooted [ˌbɛəˈfutid] *a.* 光着脚的

· 229 ·

Fifty Famous Stories Retold

The king went toward the boy. He held a gold piece in his hand.

"My boy," he said, "how would you like to have this piece of money?"

"I would like it," said the boy; "but I never hope to have so much."

"You shall have it if you will run back to the **oak**[①] tree at the second turning of the road, and fetch me the book that I left there."

The king thought that the boy would be pleased. But not so. He turned away, and said, "I am not so silly as you think."

"What do you mean?" said the king. "Who says that you are silly?"

"Well," said the boy, "you think that I am silly enough to believe that you will give me that gold piece for running a mile, and fetching you a book. You can't catch me."

"But if I give it to you now, perhaps you will believe me," said the king; and he put the gold piece into the little fellow's hand.

The boy's eyes sparkled; but he did not move.

"What is the matter now?" said the king. "Won't you go?"

The boy said, "I would like to go; but I can't leave the geese. They will **stray away**[②], and then I shall be blamed for it."

"Oh, I will tend them while you are away," said the king.

The boy laughed. "I should like to see you tending them!" he said. "Why, they would run away from you in a minute."

"Only let me try," said the king.

At last the boy gave the king his whip, and started off. He had gone but a little way, when he turned and came back.

"What is the matter now?" said Maximilian.

"**Crack**[①] the whip!"

The king tried to do as he was bidden, but he could not make a sound.

"I thought as much," said the boy. "You don't know how to do anything."

Then he took the whip, and gave the king lessons in whip cracking. "Now you see how it is done," he said, as he handed it back. "If the geese try to run away, crack it loud."

① oak [əuk] *n.* 橡树

② stray away 走失

国王走了过去，手里拿着一块金币。

"我的孩子！"国王说，"你想不想得到这块金币？"

"当然想！"男孩说，"可我从来不敢奢望能有这么多的钱！"

"你去这条路第二个拐弯处那棵橡树下面，把我掉在那里的书取回来，这个金币就归你了。"

国王原本以为男孩会十分高兴，不料那个男孩转身便走开了，说："我才没有你想的那么蠢呢！"

"你是什么意思？"国王说，"谁说你蠢啦？"

"哼，"男孩说，"你以为我这么笨，会相信跑一英里路帮你拿一本书，就会得到这块金币？我才不上当呢！"

"我现在就把金币给你，你是不是就相信了？"国王说。说完，他把金币放在小家伙的手上。

小男孩的眼睛亮了一下，可是并没有挪动脚步。

"又怎么了？"国王说，"你不愿意去吗？"

男孩说："我当然愿意去，可是我不能不管这些鹅。它们会乱跑，而我会挨骂的。"

"噢，你不在的时候，我替你照看它们。"国王说。

小孩笑了起来。"我倒想看看你是怎么照看它们的！"他说，"哼，恐怕它们马上会从你的身旁溜掉。"

"那就让我试试吧！"国王说。

男孩把鞭子交到国王的手上，就动身出发了。可是只走了一小段路，他就又转身回来了。

"又怎么了？"麦克西米利安问道。

"你要把鞭子甩响！"

国王试着照他说的试了试，可是连一点声响也弄不出来。

"我就知道，"男孩说，"你什么事也不会干。"

说完男孩拿起鞭子，教国王怎么才能把鞭子甩响。"现在你该知道怎么做了吧？"他一边说，一边把鞭子递回去。

· 231 ·

"Crack the whip!"

The king laughed. He did his best to learn his lesson; and soon the boy again started off on his errand.

Maximilian sat down on a stone, and laughed at the thought of being a goose herd. But the geese missed their master at once. With a great cackling and hissing they went, half flying, half running, across the meadow.

The king ran after them, but he could not run fast. He tried to crack the whip, but it was of no use. The geese were soon far away. What was worse, they had gotten into a garden, and were feeding on the tender vegetables.

A few minutes afterward, the goose boy came back with the book.

"Just as I thought," he said. "I have found the book, and you have lost the geese."

"Never mind," said the king, "I will help you get them again."

"Well, then, run around that way, and stand by the brook while I drive them out of the garden."

① crack [kræk] v. 使……噼啪作响

"你要把鞭子甩响!"

"如果鹅要跑,你就使劲用鞭子甩出很大的声响。"

国王笑了,并且努力学了起来。男孩又起身去执行他的任务了。

麦克西米利安坐在一块石头上面,嘲笑自己竟然变成了鹅倌。这些鹅察觉到主人不在,立刻就咯咯叽叽地叫着,连飞带跑地冲出了草地。

国王在鹅后面追,可是他跑不快。他努力想把鞭子甩响,可是也没有用,很快那些鹅就跑远了。更糟糕的是,它们居然跑到菜园子里面,吃起了蔬菜的嫩叶。

几分钟后,放鹅的孩子拿着书回来了。

"跟我刚才想的一样。"孩子说,"我找到了书,你却弄丢了鹅。"

"没关系。"国王说,"我帮你把它们再赶回来。"

"那好,你绕着那条路跑,站在小溪边上,我去把它们从菜园里面赶出来。"

The king did as he was told. The boy ran forward with his whip, and after a great deal of shouting and **scolding**①, the geese were driven back into the meadow.

"I hope you will **pardon**② me for not being a better goose herd," said Maximilian; "but, as I am a king, I am not used to such work."

"A king, indeed!" said the boy. "I was very silly to leave the geese with you. But I am not so silly as to believe that you are a king."

"Very well," said Maximilian, with a smile; "here is another gold piece, and now let us be friends."

The boy took the gold, and thanked the giver. He looked up into the king's face and said, —

"You are a very kind man, and I think you might be a good king; but if you were to try all your life, you would never be a good goose herd."

① scolding ['skəuldiŋ] *n.* 斥责

② pardon ['pɑːdn] *v.* 宽恕

　　国王照着孩子说的做了。小男孩拿着鞭子向前跑去，在一阵叫喊声和驱赶之下，鹅又被赶回到了草地上。

　　"我不是一个好鹅倌，我希望得到你的谅解。"麦克西米利安说，"我是一个国王，这样的工作我干不好。"

　　"你是国王，你骗谁呢！"男孩揶揄道，"我把鹅交给你照看就已经蠢到家了。我才不会再蠢到相信你是一个国王！"

　　"很好！"麦克西米利安一边微笑一边说，"这里还有一块金币，现在我们交个朋友吧！"

　　男孩拿起金币，向国王道着谢。他抬起头看着国王的脸，说：

　　"你是个大好人，我想你也许是一个好国王。可是这辈子不管怎样，你也无法成为一个好的鹅倌。"

45. The Inchcape Rock

In the North Sea there is a great rock called the Inchcape Rock. It is twelve miles from any land, and is covered most of the time with water.

Many boats and ships have been wrecked on that rock; for it is so near the top of the water that no vessel can sail over it without striking it.

More than a hundred years ago there lived not far away a kind-hearted man who was called the **Abbot**[1] of Aberbrothock.

"It is a pity," he said, "that so many brave sailors should lose their lives on that hidden rock."

So the abbot caused a **buoy**[2] to be fastened to the rock. The buoy floated back and forth in the shallow water. A strong chain kept it from floating away.

On the top of the buoy the abbot placed a bell; and when the waves dashed against it, the bell would ring out loud and clear.

Sailors, now, were no longer afraid to cross the sea at that place. When they heard the bell ringing, they knew just where the rock was, and they steered their vessels around it.

"God bless the good Abbot of Aberbrothock!" they all said.

45. 印奇开普暗礁

① abbot ['æbət] *n.* 男修道院院长

② buoy [bɔi] *n.* 浮标

北海里面有一块巨大的礁石，名叫印奇开普暗礁。这块礁石距离陆地十二英里，平时都淹没在海面以下。

由于礁石的顶部离水面很近，每次只要有船从上面驶过就会碰到，因此有很多大大小小的船只都曾经在这里触礁搁浅。

一百多年前，离印奇开普暗礁不远的地方住着一个心地善良的人，人们称他艾伯布洛索克修道院院长。

"太可惜了！"修道院院长说，"那么多勇敢的水手在这里失去了生命。"

于是，修道院院长派人在暗礁上安装了一个浮标。浮标漂浮在礁石上面的浅水中，还有一根结实的锁链拴着，这样就不会被海水冲走了。

修道院院长还在浮标上面放了一口钟。每当海浪冲击浮标，钟就会发出响亮而清脆的声音。

水手们现在从那片海域驶过再也不用发愁了。他们只要听到钟声响起，就能够立刻判断出暗礁的位置，并且开着船绕过那块礁石。

"愿上帝保佑仁慈的艾伯布洛索克修道院院长！"水手们都这么说。

Fifty Famous Stories Retold

One calm summer day, a ship with a black flag happened to sail not far from the Inchcape Rock. The ship belonged to a sea robber called Ralph the Rover; and she was a terror to all honest people both on sea and shore.

There was but little wind that day, and the sea was as smooth as glass. The ship stood almost still; there was hardly a breath of air to fill her sails.

Ralph the Rover was walking on the deck. He looked out upon the glassy sea. He saw the buoy floating above the Inchcape Rock. It looked like a big black **speck**[①] upon the water. But the bell was not ringing that day. There were no waves to set it in motion.

"Boys!" cried Ralph the Rover; "put out the boat, and row me to the Inchcape Rock. We will play a trick on the old abbot."

The boat was lowered. Strong arms soon rowed it to the Inchcape Rock. Then the robber, with a heavy ax, broke the chain that held the buoy.

He cut the fastenings of the bell. It fell into the water. There was a **gurgling**[②] sound as it sank out of sight.

"The next one that comes this way will not bless the abbot," said Ralph the Rover.

Soon a breeze sprang up, and the black ship sailed away. The sea robber laughed as he looked back and saw that there was nothing to mark the place of the hidden rock.

For many days, Ralph the Rover **scoured**[③] the seas, and many were the ships that he **plundered**[④]. At last he chanced to sail back toward the place from which he had started.

The wind had blown hard all day. The waves rolled high. The ship was moving swiftly. But in the evening the wind died away, and a thick fog came on.

Ralph the Rover walked the deck. He could not see where the ship was going. "If the fog would only clear away!" he said.

"I thought I heard the roar of breakers," said the pilot. "We must be near the shore."

① speck [spek] *n.* 斑点

② gurgling ['gə:glɪŋ] *v.* (gurgle 的现在分词) 作汩汩声

③ scour ['skauə] *v.* 荡涤, 肃清

④ plunder ['plʌndə(r)] *v.* 掠夺

一个平静的夏日，一艘挂着一面黑旗的船正好行驶到印奇开普暗礁附近。这条船的主人是一个名叫拉尔夫的海盗，无论在海上还是在陆地上，善良的人们都对他心存恐惧。

那天的风力很小，大海平静得像一面镜子，海面上难得有一丝风吹到船帆上面，海盗船停在那里几乎不动。

海盗拉尔夫走上甲板，注视着平静如镜的海面，看到了漂浮在印奇开普暗礁上的浮标。它看上去就像一块漂在水面上的黑斑，由于没有风浪，钟也没有发出一丝声响。

"弟兄们！"海盗拉尔夫叫道，"把小船放下去，把我送到印奇开普暗礁那里，我们要和老院长开个玩笑。"

小船被放了下去，水手们凭借强壮的双臂很快就划到印奇开普暗礁那里。然后，海盗拉尔夫用一把大斧头将系在浮标上的锁链砍断。

紧接着，他又砍掉了系在上面的钟，那口钟咕咚一声沉入了海中。

"下一艘从这里经过的船就不会再感谢修道院院长了。"海盗拉尔夫说。

过了一会儿，海面上起了微风，这艘黑色的海盗船开走了。转身看到那块暗礁上再也没有什么标志，海盗拉尔夫大笑了起来。

海盗拉尔夫在海上横行了多日，又抢劫了许多船只，最后正好又回到原先出发的地方。

那天，海上的狂风刮了整整一天。海面上波涛汹涌，这艘海盗船在海面上飞速行驶着。到了晚上，风渐渐平息了下来，海面上起了浓雾。

海盗拉尔夫走在甲板上，浓雾让他无法看清楚船的航向。"要是雾散了该多好啊！"他说。

"我好像听到浪花冲击暗礁的声音。"舵手说，"一

"I cannot tell," said Ralph the Rover; "but I think we are not far from the Inchcape Rock. I wish we could hear the good abbot's bell."

The next moment there was a great crash. "It is the Inchcape Rock!" the sailors cried, as the ship gave a **lurch**[1] to one side, and began to sink.

"Oh, what a **wretch**[2] am I!" cried Ralph the Rover. "This is what comes of the joke that I played on the good abbot!"

What was it that he heard as the waves rushed over him? Was it the abbot's bell, ringing for him far down at the bottom of the sea?

① lurch [lə:tʃ] *n.* 突然倾斜
② wretch [retʃ] *n.* 不幸的人

定已经靠近海岸了。"

"我分辨不出来。"海盗拉尔夫说,"不过我想我们离印奇开普暗礁已经不远,现在真希望能听到那个好心的院长的钟声。"

突然,一阵巨大的撞击声传来。"是印奇开普暗礁!"水手们叫了起来,海盗船的船身突然斜向了一边,开始下沉。

"唉,我怎么这么倒霉!"海盗拉尔夫叫道,"这就是我和善良的修道院长开玩笑的报应!"

海水从海盗海拉尔身上冲过的时候,他听到了什么?是不是修道院院长的钟,在遥远的海底深处为他敲响了?

46. Whittington and His Cat

I. THE CITY

There was once a little boy whose name was Richard Whittington; but everybody called him Dick. His father and mother had died when he was only a babe, and the people who had the care of him were very poor. Dick was not old enough to work, and so he had a hard time of it indeed. Sometimes he had no breakfast, and sometimes he had no dinner; and he was glad at any time to get a **crust**[①] of bread or a drop of milk.

Now, in the town where Dick lived, the people liked to talk about London. None of them had ever been to the great city, but they seemed to know all about the wonderful things which were to be seen there. They said that all the folks who lived in London were fine gentlemen and ladies; that there was singing and music there all day long; that nobody was ever hungry there, and nobody had to work; and that the streets were all paved with gold.

Dick listened to these stories, and wished that he could go to London.

One day a big **wagon**[②] drawn by eight horses, all with bells on their heads, drove into the little town. Dick saw the wagon standing by the **inn**[③], and he thought that it must be going to the fine city of London.

When the driver came out and was ready to start, the lad ran up and asked him if he might walk by the side of the wagon. The driver asked him some

46. 威廷顿和他的猫

（1）城市

　　从前，有一个小男孩名叫理查德·威廷顿，不过大家都叫他迪克。迪克很小的时候，爸爸妈妈就离开了人世，照顾他的人经济上也十分拮据。迪克由于年龄太小，还不能出去工作，生活过得十分清苦，有时候连吃饭都会上顿不接下顿。只要有一点面包屑①或一滴牛奶吃，迪克就会感到十分高兴。

　　迪克居住的小镇里，人们都喜欢谈论伦敦。虽然谁也没有到过伦敦，可是好像大家都熟知那里的奇妙见闻。他们说住在伦敦的人都是优雅的绅士和淑女，天天歌舞升平，那里没有饥饿，也不需要出去工作，街道上铺满了金子。

　　迪克听了这些故事，盼望着有一天自己能到伦敦去。

　　一天，一辆八匹马拉的四轮大马车②驶进了小镇，那些马的头上还挂着铃铛。迪克看见马车停在旅馆③旁边，猜想它一定是去伦敦那样的好地方的。

　　车夫出来了准备出发。迪克立刻跑过去询问车夫，可不可以让他跟着马车一起走。车夫问了迪克一些问题，

① crust [krʌst] *n.* 面包皮

② wagon ['wægən] *n.* 四轮马车
③ inn [in] *n.* 旅馆

· 243 ·

Fifty Famous Stories Retold

questions; and when he learned how poor Dick was, and that he had neither father nor mother, he told him that he might do as he liked.

It was a long walk for the little lad; but by and by he came to the city of London. He was in such a hurry to see the wonderful sights, that he forgot to thank the driver of the wagon. He ran as fast as he could, from one street to another, trying to find those that were paved with gold. He had once seen a piece of money that was gold, and he knew that it would buy a great, great many things; and now he thought that if he could get only a little bit of the pavement, he would have everything that he wanted.

Poor Dick ran till he was so tired that he could run no farther. It was growing dark, and in every street there was only dirt instead of gold. He sat down in a dark corner, and cried himself to sleep.

When he woke up the next morning, he was very hungry; but there was not even a crust of bread for him to eat. He forgot all about the golden pavements, and thought only of food. He walked about from one street to another, and at last grew so hungry that he began to ask those whom he met to give him a **penny**[①] to buy something to eat.

"Go to work, you **idle**[②] fellow," said some of them; and the rest passed him by without even looking at him.

"I wish I could go to work!" said Dick.

II. THE KITCHEN

By and by Dick grew so **faint**[③] and tired that he could go no farther. He sat down by the door of a fine house, and wished that he was back again in the little town where he was born. The cook-maid, who was just getting dinner, saw him, and called out,—

"What are you doing there, you little **beggar**[④]? If you don't get away quick, I'll throw a panful of hot dishwater over you. Then I guess you will jump."

得知他生活困窘，没有爸爸也没有妈妈，便告诉他当然没有问题。

　　对于这个孩子而言，这趟旅行真的太漫长了。但迪克最终还是到达了伦敦，他迫不及待地想去看那些美妙的景色，匆忙间竟然连向车夫道谢都忘了。迪克拼命地跑着，从一条街道跑到另一条街道，想找到那些铺着金子的道路。他以前曾经见过一枚金币，知道用它可以买到很多很多东西。迪克心想，要是现在能从铺着黄金的路面上弄到一小点金子，就可以买到他想要的所有东西了。

　　可怜的迪克不停地跑着，一直跑到再也跑不动了。天色渐渐暗了下来，可是每条街道上只有泥土没有金子。迪克坐在一个黑暗的角落里大哭了起来，哭着哭着竟然睡着了。

　　第二天早上醒来的时候，迪克觉得肚子饿得咕咕叫，可是连一点面包屑也吃不到。现在他已经顾不上再去想那些铺着金子的道路了，心里只想着食物。他从一条街道走到另一条街道，最后实在饿极了，只好向路人讨要一个便士①买点东西吃。

　　"去找活干啊，你这个懒惰②的家伙！"一些人说道。还有些人从迪克身边经过的时候，甚至连瞧都不瞧他一眼。

　　"我多么希望能找到活干！"迪克说。

（2）厨房

　　迪克渐渐觉得又虚弱③又疲惫，甚至连走路的力气也快没有了。他在一幢十分漂亮的房子前面坐了下来，心想要是现在能回他出生的那个小镇该多好。就在这时，屋里的一个厨娘看见了他，她正忙着准备晚餐。厨娘朝迪克大声喊道：

　　"你这个小乞丐④，坐在这里干什么？还不快点滚开，不要等到我用滚烫的洗碗水泼你，那时候我想你会跳起来跑掉的。"

① penny ['peni] *n.* 便士

② idle ['aidl] *a.* 懒惰的

③ faint ['feint] *a.* 虚弱的

④ beggar ['begə] *n.* 乞丐

Just at that time the master of the house, whose name was Mr. Fitzwarren, came home to dinner. When he saw the **ragged**① little fellow at his door, he said, —

"My lad, what are you doing here? I am afraid you are a lazy fellow, and that you want to live without work."

"No, indeed!" said Dick. "I would like to work, if I could find anything to do. But I do not know anybody in this town, and I have not had anything to eat for a long time."

"Poor little fellow!" said Mr. Fitzwarren. "Come in, and I will see what I can do for you." And he ordered the cook to give the lad a good dinner, and then to find some light work for him to do.

Little Dick would have been very happy in the new home which he had thus found, if it had not been for the cross cook. She would often say,—

"You are my boy now, and so you must do as I tell you. Look sharp there! Make the fires, carry out the ashes, wash these dishes, sweep the floor, bring in the wood! Oh, what a lazy fellow you are!" And then she would **box**② his ears, or beat him with the broomstick.

At last, little Alice, his master's daughter, saw how he was treated, and she told the cook she would be turned off if she was not kinder to the lad. After that, Dick had an easier time of it; but his troubles were not over yet, **by any means**③.

His bed was in a **garret**④ at the top of the house, far away from the rooms where the other people slept. There were many holes in the floor and walls, and every night a great number of rats and mice came in. They **tormented**⑤ Dick so much, that he did not know what to do.

One day a gentleman gave him a penny for cleaning his shoes, and he made up his mind that he would buy a cat with it. The very next morning he met a girl who was carrying a cat in her arms.

"I will give you a penny for that cat," he said.

"All right," the girl said. "You may have her, and you will find that she is a good mouser too."

① ragged ['rægid] *a.* 衣衫褴褛的

② box [bɔks] *v.* 打耳光

③ by any means 无论如何
④ garret ['gærət] *n.* 阁楼

⑤ torment [tɔː'ment] *v.* 折磨

碰巧这时候房子的主人菲茨瓦伦先生回家吃晚饭，看到这个衣衫褴褛的小家伙坐在家门口，便问道：

"我的孩子，你在这里做什么？你是不是个懒家伙，想不劳而获？"

"不，不是的！"迪克回答说，"只要能够找到事情做，我很愿意工作。可是在这里我一个人也不认识，我已经好久没吃东西了。"

"可怜的小家伙！"菲茨瓦伦先生说，"进来吧，让我看看能为你做些什么。"他马上让厨师给这个孩子做了一顿丰盛的晚餐，还在家里找了一些轻松的活让他干。

如果不是那个坏脾气的厨娘，也许小迪克在这个刚刚找到的新家里会过得十分愉快。这个厨娘经常说：

"你现在是我的仆人，必须按照我的吩咐去做，你要把眼睛放亮一些！去把火生着，把灰倒掉，洗碗，扫地，添柴！啊，你真是个懒家伙！"接着她就会抽迪克耳光，还拿扫帚柄打他。

后来，主人的女儿艾丽斯发现了迪克的遭遇。她便警告厨娘，如果再不对这个孩子好一点，就要炒她鱿鱼。从那以后，迪克的日子才稍稍好过了一些。可是不管怎样，麻烦事依然困扰着他。

迪克的床在房顶的阁楼里，跟其他人的卧室离得很远。阁楼的墙壁上和地板上有很多破洞，每到晚上就会有许多大大小小的老鼠跑进来，搅得迪克不得安宁。他不知道该怎么办才好。

一天，迪克给一个绅士擦鞋，那个人给了他一个便士，迪克下定决心要买一只猫。第二天早晨，他遇到一个女孩，手里刚好抱着一只猫。

"我想用一个便士买你的猫。"迪克说。

"好吧！"女孩说，"猫卖给你了，你会发现它的确是一只擅长捕鼠的好猫。"

Fifty Famous Stories Retold

Dick hid his cat in the garret, and every day he carried a part of his dinner to her. It was not long before she had driven all the rats and mice away; and then Dick could sleep soundly every night.

III. THE VENTURE

Some time after that, a ship that belonged to Mr. Fitzwarren was about to start on a voyage across the sea. It was loaded with goods which were to be sold in lands far away. Mr. Fitzwarren wanted to give his servants a chance for good fortune too, and so he called all of them into the **parlor**①, and asked if they had anything they would like to send out in the ship for trade.

Every one had something to send,—every one but Dick; and as he had neither money nor goods, he stayed in the kitchen, and did not come in with the rest. Little Alice guessed why he did not come, and so she said to her papa,—

"Poor Dick ought to have a chance too. Here is some money out of my own purse that you may **put in**② for him."

"No, no, my child!" said Mr. Fitzwarren. "He must risk something of his own." And then he called very loud, "Here, Dick! What are you going to send out on the ship?"

Dick heard him, and came into the room.

"I have nothing in the world," he said, "but a cat which I bought some time ago for a penny."

"Fetch your cat, then, my lad," said Mr. Fitzwarren, "and let her go out. Who knows but that she will bring you some profit?"

Dick, with tears in his eyes, carried poor **puss**③ down to the ship, and gave her to the captain. Everybody laughed at his queer venture; but little Alice felt sorry for him, and gave him money to buy another cat.

After that, the cook was worse than before. She made fun of him for sending his cat to sea. "Do you think," she would say, "that puss will sell for enough money to buy a stick to beat you?"

At last Dick could not stand her **abuse**④ any longer, and he made up his mind

迪克把猫藏在阁楼里面，每天从自己的食物里面分一些给它吃。没过多长时间，猫就把那些老鼠全都赶走了。于是，迪克每天晚上都可以睡得十分安稳。

（3）投资

一段时间之后，菲茨瓦伦先生的船准备出海，那艘船上载满了货物准备运到很远的地方出售，菲茨瓦伦先生没有忘记给仆人们提供一个赚钱的好机会。他把大家召集到客厅里面，问他们有没有东西要一起带出去出售。

每个仆人都有东西要送出去，只有迪克没有。他没有钱也没有东西，只好待在厨房里，没有跟其他人一起去客厅。小艾丽丝猜到了迪克没来的原因，便对爸爸说：

"可怜的迪克也应该有一个机会。我的钱袋里还有一些钱，你拿去给他作投资吧！"

"不，不，我的孩子！"菲茨瓦伦先生说，"迪克一定要用自己的东西去冒险。"说完他大声喊道："过来，迪克！你准备把什么东西送到船上去？"

迪克听到菲茨瓦伦先生叫他，便走进了客厅。

"我只有一只猫，是我不久前花一便士买的。"他说，"除此之外，我在这个世界上一无所有。"

"那就把你的猫拿来，我的孩子。"菲茨瓦伦先生说，"让它去吧，谁知道它能不能给你带来收益呢？"

迪克眼含泪水，把那只可怜的猫送到船上交给船长。大家都在嘲笑他这个奇怪的投资，只有小艾丽丝为他感到难过。她又给迪克一些钱让他再去买一只猫。

从那以后厨娘变得更凶了，她嘲笑迪克把猫送到海上去。"你想想，"她说，"卖猫的钱，够不够买一根棍子打你？"

后来，迪克再也无法忍受厨娘的虐待，准备返回小

① parlor ['pɑ:lə] *n.* 客厅

② put in 投资

③ puss [pus] *n.* 猫咪

④ abuse [ə'bju:s] *n.* 虐待

to go back to his old home in the little country town. So, very early in the morning on **Allhallows**[1] Day, he started. He walked as far as the place called Holloway, and there he sat down on a stone, which to this day is called "Whittington's Stone."

As he sat there very sad, and wondering which way he should go, he heard the bells on Bow Church, far away, ringing out a merry **chime**[2]. He listened. They seemed to say to him,—

"Turn again, Whittington, **thrice**[3] Lord Mayor of London."

"Well, well!" he said to himself. "I would put up with almost anything, to be Lord Mayor of London when I am a man, and to ride in a fine coach! I think I will go back and let the old cook **cuff**[4] and scold as much as she pleases."

Dick did go back, and he was lucky enough to get into the kitchen, and set about his work, before the cook came downstairs to get breakfast.

IV. THE CAT

Mr. Fitzwarren's ship made a long voyage, and at last reached a strange land on the other side of the sea. The people had never seen any white men before, and they came in great crowds to buy the fine things with which the

① Allhallows [ˌɔl'hæləuz] *n.* 万圣节

② chime [tʃaim] *n.* 钟声

③ thrice [θrais] *ad.* 三次

④ cuff [kʌf] v 用巴掌打

镇上原来的那个家。万圣节的那天早晨迪克出发了，他一口气走到一个叫作好乐威的地方，才坐在一块石头上休息。那块石头就是现在的"威廷顿石"。

迪克坐在石头上，心里感到非常难过，不知道下面该往哪里去。突然，远处的教堂响起了欢乐的钟声，迪克仔细聆听着，觉得钟声好像在对他说：

"还是回去吧，威廷顿，今后你要三次出任伦敦市的市长。"

"好！好！"迪克自言自语道，"我一定要忍受所有的磨难，长大后要做伦敦市的市长，坐漂亮的马车。我想还是回去吧，随便那个老厨娘怎么打骂都行。"

迪克转身往回走去。他十分幸运，厨娘当时还没下楼做早餐。他溜进厨房里面，便开始忙了起来。

（4）猫

菲茨瓦伦先生的船经过漫长的航行，抵达了海洋彼岸一个陌生的地方。住在那里的人以前从未见过白种人，他们蜂拥而来，想买船上的那些好东西。船长很想和这

ship was loaded. The captain wanted very much to trade with the king of the country; and it was not long before the king sent word for him to come to the palace and see him.

The captain did so. He was shown into a beautiful room, and given a seat on a rich carpet all flowered with silver and gold. The king and queen were seated not far away; and soon a number of dishes were brought in for dinner.

They had hardly begun to eat when an army of rats and mice rushed in, and **devoured**[1] all the meat before any one could hinder them. The captain wondered at this, and asked if it was not very unpleasant to have so many rats and mice about.

"Oh, yes!" was the answer. "It is indeed unpleasant; and the king would give half his treasure if he could get rid of them."

The captain jumped for joy. He remembered the cat which little Whittington had sent out; and he told the king that he had a little creature on board his ship which would make short work of the pests.

Then it was the king's turn to jump for joy; and he jumped so high, that his yellow cap, or turban, dropped off his head.

"Bring the creature to me," he said. "If she will do what you say, I will load your ship with gold."

The captain **made believe**[2] that he would be very sorry to part with the cat; but at last he went down to the ship to get her, while the king and queen made haste to have another dinner made ready.

The captain, with puss under his arm, reached the palace just in time to see the table crowded with rats. The cat leaped out upon them, and oh! What **havoc**[3] she did make among the troublesome creatures! Most of them were soon stretched dead upon the floor, while the rest **scampered**[4] away to their holes, and did not dare to come out again.

The king had never been so glad in his life; and the queen asked that the creature which had done such wonders should be brought to her. The captain called, "Pussy, pussy, pussy!" and the cat came up and rubbed against his legs.

个国家的国王做生意，很快国王派人捎来口信，让他去王宫见面。

船长来到王宫，被带到一间漂亮的房子里面。他坐在用金丝银线绣成的漂亮花地毯上，国王和王后就在不远处落座。很快，许多好吃的东西被端了上来，宴会开始了。

可是就在他们准备用餐的时候，一大群老鼠冲了进来。人们阻拦不及，不一会儿它们很快就把那些佳肴吃了个精光。船长感到十分诧异，他问有这么多老鼠，难道他们不觉得难受吗？

"难受！"有人回答说，"实在太可恶了，如果有人能除掉这些老鼠，国王愿意拿出一半财产给他。"

船长高兴得跳了起来，他想起了小威廷顿的那只猫。他告诉国王船上有一只小动物，可以很快把这些害人的家伙消灭掉。

这回换成是国王高兴得跳了起来。他跳得老高，头上戴的黄色头巾帽子都掉了下来。

"快去把那个动物给我带来。"国王说，"如果它真的像你说的那样，我就要把你的船装满黄金。"

船长假装很不舍得那只猫。不过他最终还是到船上取猫，国王和王后则是迅速准备了另一桌筵席。

船长带着猫返回王宫，正好看见桌子上又挤满老鼠，猫立刻跳上去捉它们。啊！对于那些讨厌的家伙而言，这是何等的灾难啊！很快，很多老鼠被咬死在地上，剩下的那些都惊慌失措地逃回洞里，再也不敢出来了。

国王这辈子都没有这么高兴过，王后让人把那只创造了奇迹的动物带到她的面前。船长叫道："猫咪，猫咪，猫咪！"猫便走上前去，在他的腿上来回蹭着。船长抓住猫，把它献给王后。王后刚开始还有点害怕，不敢去碰猫。

① devour [di'vauə] v. 吞食

② make believe 假装

③ havoc ['hævək] n. 浩劫

④ scamper ['skæmpə] v. 惊惶奔跑

He picked her up, and offered her to the queen; but at first the queen was afraid to touch her.

However, the captain stroked the cat, and called, "Pussy, pussy, pussy!" and then the queen ventured to touch her. She could only say, "Putty, putty, putty!" for she had not learned to talk English. The captain then put the cat down on the queen's lap, where she **purred**[①] and purred until she went to sleep.

The king would not have missed getting the cat now **for the world**[②]. He at once made a bargain with the captain for all the goods on board the ship; and then he gave him ten times as much for the cat as all the rest came to.

The captain was very glad. He bade the king and queen goodbye, and the very next day set sail for England.

V. THE FORTUNE

One morning Mr. Fitzwarren was sitting at his desk in his office. He heard some one tap softly at his door, and he said, —

"Who's there?"

"A friend," was the answer. "I have come to bring you news of your ship 'Unicorn.'"

Mr. Fitzwarren jumped up quickly, and opened the door. Whom should he seen waiting there but the captain, with a bill of lading in one hand and a box of jewels in the other? He was so full of joy that he lifted up his eyes, and thanked Heaven for sending him such good fortune.

The captain soon told the story of the cat; and then he showed the rich present which the king and queen had sent to poor Dick in payment for her. As soon as the good gentleman heard this, he called out to his servants, —

"Go send him in, and tell him of his fame; pray call him Mr. Whittington by name."

Some of the men who stood by said that so great a present ought not to be given to a mere boy; but Mr. Fitzwarren frowned upon them.

"It is his own," he said, "and I will not hold back one penny from him."

① purr [pə:] v.（猫）发低而持续的呼噜声
② for the world（否定句内）无论如何

于是船长一边轻轻地抚摸着猫，一边嘴里叫着："猫咪，猫咪，猫咪！"王后的胆子这才大了起来。她还没有学会英语，只会说："喵，喵，喵！"接着，船长把猫放到王后的膝盖上，这只猫咕噜咕噜地叫着，很快就在那里睡着了。

国王无论如何不愿意错过得到这只猫的机会。他立刻和船长商定买下整船的货物，并且出了高于那些货物十倍的价钱买下那只猫。

船长高兴坏了。第二天，他便向国王和王后道别，起航返回英格兰。

（5）好运

一天清晨，菲茨瓦伦先生正坐在办公室的书桌旁，忽然听到有人轻轻敲门。他问：

"是谁？"

"一个朋友。"那人回答说，"我给您带来了'独角兽'号的消息。"

菲茨瓦伦先生马上起身去开门。他看见站在门口的不是别人，正是船长，他一手拿着一张货物的清单，一手提着一个珠宝箱。船长实在太兴奋了，眼睛不停地往天上看，他在感谢上帝赐予他这么好的运气。

船长立刻向菲茨瓦伦先生汇报了那只猫的故事，还拿出了很多贵重的礼物，它们都是国王和王后作为猫的报酬送给可怜的迪克的。这位仁慈的绅士听到这个消息后，马上对仆人喊道：

"快去把迪克叫来，告诉他这些荣誉，请尊称他威廷顿先生。"

站在一旁的几个人说，不应该把这么贵重的礼物交给一个小男孩，菲茨瓦伦先生皱了皱眉头表示反对。

"这理当是他的东西。"菲茨瓦伦先生说："我一个便士也不会留。"

Fifty Famous Stories Retold

Dick was scouring the pots when word was brought to him that he should go to the office.

"Oh, I am so dirty!" he said, "and my shoes are full of hobnails." But he was told to make haste.

Mr. Fitzwarren ordered a chair to be set for him, and then the lad began to think that they were making fun of him.

"I beg that you won't play tricks with a poor boy like me," he said. "Please let me go back to my work."

"Mr. Whittington," said Mr. Fitzwarren, "this is no joke at all. The captain has sold your cat, and has brought you, in return for her, more riches than I have in the whole world."

Then he opened the box of jewels, and showed Dick his treasures.

The poor boy did not know what to do. He begged his master to take a part of it; but Mr. Fitzwarren said, "No, it is all your own; and I feel sure that you will make good use of it."

Dick then offered some of his jewels to his mistress and little Alice. They thanked him, and told him that they felt great joy at his good luck, but wished him to keep his riches for himself.

传话的人叫迪克到办公室去，当时他正在厨房里面洗锅。

　　"啊，我太脏了！"迪克说，"我的鞋子也太破了，上面都是补过的鞋钉。"但是来人催促他要快点过去。

　　菲茨瓦伦先生叫人搬来一把椅子让迪克坐下。刚开始的时候，这孩子觉得他们一定是在和他开玩笑。

　　"请不要捉弄像我这样的穷孩子吧！"迪克说，"我还要回去继续干活！"

　　"威廷顿先生，"菲茨瓦伦先生说，"这根本不是玩笑。船长把你的猫卖了，报酬也给你带回来了，那笔钱比我所有财富加起来还要多。"

　　说完，菲茨瓦伦先生打开了珠宝箱，把里面的金银珠宝给迪克看。

　　这个可怜的孩子一时不知道该怎么办，恳求主人留下一部分珠宝。可是菲茨瓦伦先生说："不，这都是你的东西，我知道你会好好利用它们的。"

　　于是，迪克拿出一些珠宝送给女主人和小艾丽丝。她们向他表示感谢，并且为他的好运气感到十分高兴，可是她们仍然希望迪克能够自己留下那些财富。

But he was too kindhearted to keep everything for himself. He gave nice presents to the captain and the sailors, and to the servants in Mr. Fitzwarren's house. He even remembered the cross old cook.

After that, Whittington's face was washed, and his hair curled, and he was dressed in a nice suit of clothes; and then he was as handsome a young man as ever walked the streets of London.

Some time after that, there was a fine wedding at the finest church in London; and Miss Alice became the wife of Mr. Richard Whittington. And the lord mayor was here, and the great judges, and the sheriffs, and many rich merchants; and everybody was very happy.

And Richard Whittington became a great merchant, and was one of the foremost men in London. He was sheriff of the city, and thrice lord mayor; and King Henry V. made him a knight.

He built the famous prison of Newgate in London. On the archway in front of the prison was a figure, cut in stone, of Sir Richard Whittington and his cat; and for three hundred years this figure was shown to all who visited London.

迪克心地十分善良，不愿意一个人独享一切。他拿出一些漂亮的礼物分别送给船长、水手和菲茨瓦伦家的仆人，就连那个坏脾气的老厨娘也得到了礼物。

从那以后，威廷顿洗干净脸，烫了头发，穿上了华丽的衣服。走在伦敦的街头，他变成了一个风度翩翩的英俊少年。

几年之后，伦敦最漂亮的教堂里举行了一场盛大的婚礼。艾丽斯小姐成为理查德·威廷顿的妻子，出席婚礼的人里面有伦敦市市长、大法官和郡长以及很多富商，大家都感到十分开心。

理查德·威廷顿后来成为一位了不起的商人，是伦敦市最杰出的人物之一。他曾经担任过城里的郡长，还出任过三次伦敦市市长，亨利五世国王册封他为爵士。

迪克在伦敦修建了著名的纽盖特监狱。今天，监狱前面的门廊上还立着一座石像，上面刻着理查德·威廷顿先生和他的猫。三百多年来，凡是到伦敦参观的人，都能够看到那座雕像。

47. Casabianca

There was a great battle at sea. One could hear nothing but the roar of the big guns. The air was filled with black smoke. The water was strewn with broken masts and pieces of timber which the cannon balls had knocked from the ships. Many men had been killed, and many more had been wounded.

The flagship had taken fire. The flames were breaking out from below. The deck was all **ablaze**[①]. The men who were left alive made haste to launch a small boat. They leaped into it, and rowed swiftly away. Any other place was safer now than on board of that burning ship. There was powder in the hold.

But the captain's son, young Casabianca, still stood upon the deck. The flames were almost all around him now; but he would not stir from his post. His father had bidden him stand there, and he had been taught always to obey. He trusted in his father's word, and believed that when the right time came he would tell him to go.

He saw the men leap into the boat. He heard them call to him to come. He shook his head.

"When father bids me, I will go," he said.

And now the flames were leaping up the masts. The sails were all ablaze. The fire blew hot upon his cheek. It **scorched**[②] his hair. It was before him, behind him, all around him.

47. 卡萨比安卡

①ablaze [əˈbleɪz] a. 着火的

②scorch [skɔːtʃ] v. 烧焦

  海面上爆发了一场激战。炮声震耳欲聋，空气中硝烟弥漫，水面上漂满了被炮弹打断的船桅和木头的碎片。许多人在战斗中失去了生命，还有更多人因此负了伤。

  领头的旗舰燃起了大火，火焰从船舱中直往上蹿，甲板上一片火光。那些幸存下来的人匆忙放下小船，跳上去飞快地逃走了。现在，无论什么地方都比这艘燃烧着的船更安全，因为船里面还装着炸药。

  船长的儿子年轻的卡萨比安卡依然坚守在甲板上面，熊熊的火焰几乎已经将他团团围住。父亲吩咐他坚守岗位，而且父亲总教导他要服从命令。卡萨比安卡对父亲说的话深信不疑，他相信在适当的时刻，父亲一定会下令让他离开的。

  卡萨比安卡看到人们跳上小船，听见他们喊他一起走，可是他都摇头拒绝了。

  "父亲让我走，我才会走。"卡萨比安卡说。

  火焰已经窜上了桅杆，整个船帆都烧了起来。大火灼热了卡萨比安卡的脸颊，烧焦了他的头发，火焰将他团团围住。

· 261 ·

"O father!" he cried, "may I not go now? The men have all left the ship. Is it not time that we too should leave it?"

He did not know that his father was lying in the burning cabin below, that a cannon ball had struck him dead at the very beginning of the fight. He listened to hear his answer.

"Speak louder, father!" he cried. "I cannot hear what you say."

Above the roaring of the flames, above the crashing of the falling spars, above the booming of the guns, he fancied that his father's voice came faintly to him through the scorching air.

"I am here, father! Speak once again!" he gasped.

But what is that?

A great flash of light fills the air; clouds of smoke shoot quickly upward to the sky; and —

"Boom!"

Oh, what a terrific sound! Louder than thunder, louder than the roar of all the guns! The air quivers; the sea itself trembles; the sky is black.

The blazing ship is seen no more.

There was powder in the hold!

* * * *

A long time ago a lady, whose name was Mrs. Hemans, wrote a poem about this brave boy Casabianca. It is not a very well written poem, and yet everybody has read it, and thousands of people have learned it by heart. I doubt not but that some day you too will read it. It begins in this way:—

"The boy stood on the burning deck
Whence all but him had fled;

"父亲！"卡萨比安卡大声喊着，"现在可以走吗？所有人都走了，难道还没有到我们撤退的时间吗？"

卡萨比安卡不知道父亲此刻正躺在燃烧着的船舱里面。战斗刚一打响，他就被一颗炮弹击中毙命，可卡萨比安卡此刻还在等待父亲的回答。

"声音再大一些，父亲！"卡萨比安卡喊道，"我听不见你说话。"

火焰的咆哮声夹杂着桅樯倒塌的爆裂声和大炮的轰隆声，恍惚中卡萨比安卡仿佛听到父亲微弱的声音穿过灼热的空气传了过来。

"我在这里，父亲！你再说一遍！"卡萨比安卡喘着气喊道。

可是那是什么？

突然，一道强光映红了天际，浓烟迅速冲上了云霄。

"轰！"

啊，多么恐怖的一声巨响！它比雷声还要响，压过了所有大炮的轰鸣！空气和大海一起颤抖着，天空突然暗了下来。

那艘燃烧着的大船已经消失得无影无踪了。

船舱里面还装着炸药！

* * * * *

很久以前，有一位名叫希曼斯夫人的女士，她写了一首描写卡萨比安卡英勇事迹的诗。那首诗虽然写得不算出色，可是几乎人人都读过它，成千上万的人还把它熟记于心，我深信有一天你们也会读到它。那首诗的开头是这样的：

"熊熊燃烧的甲板之上，

> The flame that lit the battle's wreck
>   Shone round him o'er the dead.
>
> "Yet beautiful and bright he stood,
>   As born to rule the storm—
> A creature of heroic blood,
>   A proud though childlike form."

只有男孩依然站在那里坚守，
火焰映红了战船的残骸，
照亮了身边战士的遗体。

"而他却依然坚定地站立着，
好像生来就要驾驭那暴风骤雨，
一个热血沸腾的英雄，
一个年轻却骄傲的身影。"

Fifty Famous Stories Retold

48. Antonio Canova

A good many years ago there lived in Italy a little boy whose name was Antonio Canova. He lived with his grandfather, for his own father was dead. His grandfather was a stonecutter, and he was very poor.

Antonio was a **puny**① lad, and not strong enough to work. He did not care to play with the other boys of the town. But he liked to go with his grandfather to the stoneyard. While the old man was busy, cutting and trimming the great blocks of stone, the lad would play among the **chips**②. Sometimes he would make a little statue of soft clay; sometimes he would take **hammer**③ and **chisel**④, and try to cut a statue from a piece of rock. He showed so much skill that his grandfather was delighted.

"The boy will be a sculptor some day," he said.

Then when they went home in the evening, the grandmother would say, "What have you been doing today, my little sculptor?"

And she would take him upon her lap and sing to him, or tell him stories that filled his mind with pictures of wonderful and beautiful things. And the next day, when he went back to the stoneyard, he would try to make some of those pictures in stone or clay.

There lived in the same town a rich man who was called the Count. Sometimes the Count would have a grand dinner, and his rich friends from other towns would

48. 安东尼奥·卡诺瓦

① puny ['pju:ni] a. 弱小的

② chip [tʃip] n. 薄片，碎块
③ hammer ['hæmə] n. 铁锤
④ chisel ['tʃizəl] n. 凿子

许多年前，意大利有一个名叫安东尼奥·卡诺瓦的小男孩。父亲去世后，他就一直跟着祖父一起生活。安东尼奥的祖父是一个石匠，家里几乎一贫如洗。

由于身体比较瘦小，安东尼奥不能去外面工作。他也不喜欢跟镇上的小孩们玩，却喜欢跟着祖父一起去采石场。老人家忙着切割修整大石头的时候，安东尼奥就会在碎石中间玩耍，有时候他会用泥巴捏一个小人，有时拿着锤子和凿子在石头上雕刻。安东尼奥的手很巧，祖父为此感到十分高兴。

"这个孩子长大了一定会成为一个雕刻家。"祖父说。

每天傍晚回到家，祖母都会问安东尼奥："我的小雕刻家，你今天又做什么了？"

然后祖母就会把安东尼奥抱到膝盖上给他唱歌，给他讲故事，这时他的脑海里便会浮现出各种各样奇妙美丽的图画。第二天回到采石场，安东尼奥就会用泥巴或者石头把那些图像呈现出来。

在他们居住的小镇上，有一个被称为伯爵的有钱人。伯爵家里有时候举行盛大的宴会，他的那些有钱的

· 267 ·

Fifty Famous Stories Retold

come to visit him. Then Antonio's grandfather would go up to the Count's house to help with the work in the kitchen; for he was a fine cook as well as a good stonecutter.

It happened one day that Antonio went with his grandfather to the Count's great house. Some people from the city were coming, and there was to be a grand feast. The boy could not cook, and he was not old enough to wait on the table; but he could wash the pans and kettles, and as he was smart and quick, he could help in many other ways.

All went well until it was time to spread the table for dinner. Then there was a crash in the dining room, and a man rushed into the kitchen with some pieces of marble in his hands. He was pale, and trembling with fright.

"What shall I do? What shall I do?" he cried. "I have broken the statue that was to stand at the center of the table. I cannot make the table look pretty without the statue. What will the Count say?"

And now all the other servants were in trouble. Was the dinner to be a failure after all? For everything depended on having the table nicely arranged. The Count would be very angry.

"Ah, what shall we do?" they all asked.

Then little Antonio Canova left his pans and kettles, and went up to the man who had caused the trouble.

"If you had another statue, could you arrange the table?" he asked.

"Certainly," said the man; "that is, if the statue were of the right length and height."

"Will you let me try to make one?" asked Antonio "Perhaps I can make something that will do."

The man laughed.

"**Nonsense**[①]!" he cried. "Who are you, that you talk of making statues **on an hour's notice**[②]?"

朋友便会从各地赶来拜访他。每到这个时候,安东尼奥的祖父就要去伯爵家的厨房帮忙。祖父不仅是一名了不起的石匠,而且还是一名出色的厨师。

一天,安东尼奥正好跟随祖父一同前往伯爵家。客人们正在从城里面赶来,一场盛大的宴会马上就要开始。安东尼奥不会做饭,而且年纪也小,无法到餐桌前服侍客人,可是他可以洗锅刷壶,再加上他那么聪明敏捷,可以帮着干很多事情。

宴会的菜肴摆上桌子之前,一切都进展得十分顺利。突然,餐厅里面传来东西打碎的声音,紧接着有个人手里拿着一些大理石的碎片冲进了厨房,因为害怕而脸色苍白,浑身发抖。

"我该怎么办?怎么办?"他喊道,"我打碎了放在桌子中间的雕像。没有雕像,就没有办法把桌子布置得好看,伯爵会怎么说我?"

当时仆人们都在发愁。餐桌布置的美观至关重要,难道晚宴就要这样被搞砸了吗?如果这件事让伯爵知道了,他一定会非常生气。

"天啊,我们该怎么办?"仆人们都在问。

就在这个时候,小安东尼奥·卡诺瓦放下手里的锅和水壶,跑到那个惹了麻烦的人面前。

"要是再有一个雕像,你是不是就可以布置餐桌了?"安东尼奥问。

"当然了!"那个人说,"只要雕像的尺寸正好合适。"

"能不能让我试着做一个?"安东尼奥问,"或许我能够做一个合适的东西出来。"

那个人笑了起来。

"胡说八道!"他叫道,"你以为你是谁?居然夸口说一小时之内就能做好一个雕像。"

---

① nonsense ['nɔnsəns] *n.* 胡说
② on...notice 提前……通知,预告

269

"I am Antonio Canova," said the lad.

"Let the boy try what he can do," said the servants, who knew him.

And so, since nothing else could be done, the man allowed him to try.

On the kitchen table there was a large square **lump**① of yellow butter. Two hundred pounds the lump weighed, and it had just come in, fresh and clean, from the dairy on the mountain. With a kitchen knife in his hand, Antonio began to cut and carve this butter. In a few minutes he had **molded**② it into the shape of a crouching lion; and all the servants crowded around to see it.

"How beautiful!" they cried. "It is a great deal prettier than the statue that was broken."

When it was finished, the man carried it to its place.

"The table will be handsomer by half than I ever hoped to make it," he said.

When the Count and his friends came in to dinner, the first thing they saw was the yellow lion.

"What a beautiful work of art!" they cried. "None but a very great artist

"The servants crowded around to see it."

① lump [lʌmp] *n.* 块

② mold [məuld] *v.* 塑造

"我是安东尼奥·卡诺瓦。"这孩子回答说。

"就让那个孩子试试吧！"认识安东尼奥的仆人们说道。

由于没有别的办法，那个人只好答应让安东尼奥试一试。

厨房的桌子上放着一块重达两百磅的方形黄色牛油，既新鲜又干净，是山上的牛奶场刚刚送来的。安东尼奥手拿厨刀，开始雕刻那块黄色的牛油。几分钟之后，一头伏狮的模样便跃然出现，仆人们都围过去想一睹为快。

"简直太漂亮了！"他们惊叹道，"比打碎的那个还要好看很多。"

狮子雕刻完后，那个人把它拿去摆在桌子原来的位置上。

"这张桌子比我预想的还要漂亮很多！"这个人说。

伯爵和他的朋友们走进餐厅，一眼就看见了那只黄色的狮子。

"多么精美绝伦的艺术品！"他们惊叹道，"只有

"仆人们都围过去想一睹为快。"

could ever carve such a figure; and how odd that he should choose to make it of butter!" And then they asked the Count to tell them the name of the artist.

"Truly, my friends," he said, "this is as much of a surprise to me as to you." And then he called to his head servant, and asked him where he had found so wonderful a statue.

"It was carved only an hour ago by a little boy in the kitchen," said the servant.

This made the Count's friends wonder still more; and the Count bade the servant call the boy into the room.

"My lad," he said, "you have done a piece of work of which the greatest artists would be proud. What is your name, and who is your teacher?"

"My name is Antonio Canova," said the boy, "and I have had no teacher but my grandfather the stonecutter."

By this time all the guests had crowded around Antonio. There were famous artists among them, and they knew that the lad was a genius. They could not say enough in praise of his work; and when at last they sat down at the table, nothing would please them but that Antonio should have a seat with them; and the dinner was made a feast in his honor.

The very next day the Count sent for Antonio to come and live with him. The best artists in the land were employed to teach him the art in which he had shown so much skill; but now, instead of carving butter, he chiseled marble. In a few years, Antonio Canova became known as one of the greatest sculptors in the world.

出色的艺术家才能做出这样的雕像。真奇怪，他竟然会选择用牛油做雕刻的材料！"说完，他们纷纷向伯爵打听这个艺术家的名字。

"说实话，我的朋友们，"伯爵说，"我和你们一样感到惊奇。"接着他让人去把仆人的领班叫来，询问领班是在哪里找到这个美妙的雕像的。

"这是一个小男孩一小时前在厨房里面刚刚完成的。"领班回答说。

伯爵的朋友们愈加感到惊奇了。于是，伯爵让领班把那个小男孩带到房间里面。

"我的孩子，"伯爵说，"你创作了一件连最伟大的艺术家都会感到骄傲的作品。你叫什么名字？你的老师是谁？"

"我的名字叫安东尼奥·卡诺瓦，"男孩说，"我没有别的老师，我祖父就是我的老师，他是一名石匠。"

这时，所有客人都跑过来把安东尼奥围了起来，他们中间还有几位是著名的艺术家，他们断定这个孩子是一个天才，对他的作品赞不绝口。随后他们坐下来开始用餐，还非要把安东尼奥叫来跟他们一起坐，最后晚餐竟然变成了安东尼奥的庆贺宴会。

第二天，伯爵就派人把安东尼奥接过来和他一起住，还请来当地最好的艺术家，给已经显露出非凡才华的安东尼奥传授雕刻的技艺。现在安东尼奥用不着再用牛油雕刻，他可以在大理石上雕刻了。几年之后，安东尼奥成为世界上最著名的雕刻家之一。

49. Picciola

Many years ago there was a poor gentleman shut up in one of the great prisons of France. His name was Charney, and he was very sad and unhappy. He had been put into prison wrongfully, and it seemed to him as though there was no one in the world who cared for him.

He could not read, for there were no books in the prison. He was not allowed to have pens or paper, and so he could not write. The time dragged slowly by. There was nothing that he could do to make the days seem shorter. His only pastime was walking back and forth in the paved prison yard. There was no work to be done, no one to talk with.

One fine morning in spring, Charney was taking his walk in the yard. He was counting the paving stones, as he had done a thousand times before. All at once he stopped. What had made that little mound of earth between two of the stones?

He stooped down to see. A seed of some kind had fallen between the stones. It had sprouted; and now a tiny green leaf was pushing its way up out of the ground. Charney was about to crush it with his foot, when he saw that there was a kind of soft coating over the leaf.

"Ah!" said he. "This coating is to keep it safe. I must not harm it." And he went on with his walk.

The next day he almost stepped upon the plant before he thought of it. He

49．皮丘拉

许多年前，有一个名叫沙尔内的可怜绅士被关进法国的一座大牢里面，他为此感到十分伤心和难过。沙尔内是蒙冤入狱的，因此他感觉世界上似乎再也没有人关心他了。

沙尔内不能看书，也不能写作，因为监狱里面没有书，也不允许犯人有笔和纸。时间过得很慢，没有什么事情可以让沙尔内消磨光阴。他唯一的消遣方式是在监狱铺过地面的院子里面来回散步，除此之外便无所事事，而且也没有人可以说话。

在一个阳光明媚的春日早晨，沙尔内正在院子里面散步；他跟往常一样，一边走一边数着铺在地上的石头。突然，他停了下来，看见两块石头中间好像顶出了一座小土堆。

沙尔内蹲下身子，发现一粒不知名的植物种子落在石头中间的泥土里面已经发了芽，一片细小的嫩叶正在破土而出。要不是看见叶子上面那层柔软的薄膜，沙尔内的脚差一点就要踩到上面。

"啊！"沙尔内说，"这层膜是保护它的，我不能伤害它。"说完，他又继续散步着。

第二天，沙尔内再次想起那棵植物的时候，脚几乎

stooped to look at it. There were two leaves now, and the plant was much stronger and greener than it was the day before. He stayed by it a long time, looking at all its parts.

Every morning after that, Charney went at once to his little plant. He wanted to see if it had been chilled by the cold, or scorched by the sun. He wanted to see how much it had grown.

One day as he was looking from his window, he saw the jailer go across the yard. The man brushed so close to the little plant, that it seemed as though he would crush it. Charney trembled from head to foot.

"O my Picciola!" he cried.

When the jailer came to bring his food, he begged the **grim**① fellow to spare his little plant. He expected that the man would laugh at him; but although a jailer, he had a kind heart.

"Do you think that I would hurt your little plant?" he said. "No, indeed! It would have been dead long ago, if I had not seen that you thought so much of it."

"That is very good of you, indeed," said Charney. He felt half ashamed at having thought the jailer unkind.

Every day he watched Picciola, as he had named the plant. Every day it grew larger and more beautiful. But once it was almost broken by the huge feet of the jailer's dog. Charney's heart sank within him.

"Picciola must have a house," he said. "I will see if I can make one."

So, though the nights were chilly, he took, day by day, some part of the firewood that was allowed him, and with this he built a little house around the plant.

The plant had a thousand pretty ways which he noticed. He saw how it always bent a little toward the sun; he saw how the flowers folded their petals before a storm.

已经踩到了它。他弯下腰去看，发现它现在已经长出两片叶子，比昨天更加茁壮油绿。他站在旁边注视了许久，仔细观察着植物的每个部分。

从那以后，每天早晨沙尔内都要去看一次那棵小植物，看看它有没有被寒冷的天气冻伤，有没有被太阳晒蔫，有没有再长大一些。

一天，沙尔内正从窗户里面往外看，看见狱卒穿过院子，他的脚离那棵小植物那么近，看上去好像马上就要踩到似的。沙尔内全身颤抖了起来。

"啊，我的皮丘拉！"沙尔内叫了起来。

狱卒进来给他送饭的时候，沙尔内恳求这个板着脸的家伙放过那棵小植物。他以为那个人会嘲笑他，可没想到他虽然身为狱卒，却也有一颗善良的心。

"你以为我会伤害你的那棵小植物吗？"狱卒说，"我才不会！假如没有看到你那样呵护它，它恐怕早就被踩死了。"

"你真的太好啦！"沙尔内说。他原以为狱卒是个冷酷的家伙，现在他为自己的这个想法感到羞愧。

就这样，沙尔内每天都去看皮丘拉，这是沙尔内给小植物取的名字。小植物越长越高，越长越漂亮，可是有一次它差点就被狱卒那条狗的大爪子踩死。沙尔内的心都沉了下去。

"皮丘拉一定要有一个房子，"沙尔内说，"我看看能不能给它修一个。"

这几天晚上天气十分寒冷，可沙尔内还是一天天地把发给他取暖用的木柴节省下来，然后用这些木头给那棵植物搭建了一座小房子。

沙尔内观察到那棵植物的千姿百态，注意到它总是对着太阳微微弯腰，也看见它在暴风雨来临之前将花瓣合拢。

① grim [grim] *a.* 严肃的，无笑容的

He had never thought of such things before, and yet he had often seen whole gardens of flowers in bloom.

One day, with **soot**[①] and water he made some ink; he spread out his handkerchief for paper; he used a sharpened stick for a pen—and all for what? He felt that he must write down the doings of his little pet. He spent all his time with the plant.

"See my lord and my lady!" the jailer would say when he saw them.

As the summer passed by, Picciola grew more lovely every day. There were no fewer than thirty blossoms on its **stem**[②].

But one sad morning it began to droop. Charney did not know what to do. He gave it water, but still it drooped. The leaves were **withering**[③]. The stones of the prison yard would not let the plant live.

Charney knew that there was but one way to save his treasure. Alas! how could he hope that it might be done? The stones must be taken up at once.

But this was a thing which the jailer dared not do. The rules of the prison were strict, and no stone must be moved. Only the highest officers in the land could have such a thing done.

Poor Charney could not sleep. Picciola must die. Already the flowers had withered; the leaves would soon fall from the stem.

Then a new thought came to Charney. He would ask the great Napoleon, the emperor himself, to save his plant.

It was a hard thing for Charney to do,—to ask a favor of the man whom he hated, the man who had shut him up in this very prison. But for the sake of Picciola he would do it.

He wrote his little story on his handkerchief. Then he gave it into the care of

① soot [suːt] *n.* 煤灰

② stem [stem] *n.*（植物的）茎

③ wither ['wiðə] *v.* 枯萎，凋谢

从前，沙尔内曾经见过满园盛开的鲜花，可是从来没有注意过这么多的细节。

一天，沙尔内用煤灰加水做墨水，用自己的手帕作纸，然后又用一支削尖的树枝作笔，他这是要干什么呢？原来，他觉得一定要把那个小宝贝的种种神态记录下来，现在他把自己所有的时间都花在这株植物上面。

"参见我的老爷和夫人！"每次狱卒看到沙尔内和那株植物都会这样说。

夏天过去了，皮丘拉长得越来越可爱，它的茎上已经开出不下三十朵花。

可是在一个让人伤心的早晨，皮丘拉开始凋谢了。沙尔内不知道该怎么办，他试着给它浇水，可它还在继续凋谢，叶子也开始枯萎，原来是监狱院子里面铺的石头妨碍了皮丘拉的生长。

沙尔内知道只有一个办法可以挽救他的宝贝。唉！可是这个办法怎样才能实现呢？这样做就需要马上把石头移开。

可是这件事连狱卒也不敢做。监狱的规定十分严格，任何人不可以随意搬动里面的石头，只有当地权力最高的长官才能够那么做。

可怜的沙尔内忧心忡忡，晚上居然连觉也睡不着。皮丘拉一定会死掉的，那些花已经枯萎了，叶子很快就要从茎上落下来。

突然，沙尔内想出了一个新主意。他想让伟大的拿破仑皇帝来救他的植物。

对于沙尔内而言，这是一件很为难的事情。如果这样，那就意味着他要去求一个自己憎恨过的人，正是这个人把他关进了监狱。可是为了挽救皮丘拉的性命，他什么也顾不得了。

沙尔内把皮丘拉的小故事写在手绢上，交给一个年

Fifty Famous Stories Retold

a young girl, who promised to carry it to Napoleon. Ah! If the poor plant would only live a few days longer!

What a long journey that was for the young girl! What a long, **dreary**① waiting it was for Charney and Picciola!

But at last news came to the prison. The stones were to be taken up. Picciola was saved!

The emperor's kind wife had heard the story of Charney's care for the plant. She saw the handkerchief on which he had written of its pretty ways.

"Surely," she said, "it can do us no good to keep such a man in prison."

And so, at last, Charney was set free. Of course he was no longer sad and unloving. He saw how God had cared for him and the little plant, and how kind and true are the hearts of even rough men. And he cherished Picciola as a dear, loved friend whom he could never forget.

轻的姑娘，姑娘答应会把手绢转交给拿破仑。啊！这株可怜的植物要是能再多活几天该多好啊！

对于这位年轻姑娘而言，这是一段多么漫长的路程啊！而对于沙尔内和皮丘拉来说，这又是一段多么漫长而忧心的等待啊！

后来，消息终于传到监狱。那块石头被移开，皮丘拉得救了！

仁慈的皇后听说了沙尔内照顾那株植物的故事，而且从写在手帕上面的文字中看到了皮丘拉千姿百态的倩影。

"说实话，"皇后说，"把这样的人关进监狱，对我们来说是没有什么益处的。"

于是沙尔内被释放了，他不用再感到悲伤和难过。他懂得了上帝是怎样爱护他和他的小植物的，而且即便是粗鲁的人，心地也可以那般善良和真诚。沙尔内照顾皮丘拉就像照顾一个亲爱的朋友一样，他永远也不会忘记它。

① dreary ['driəri] *a.* 沉闷的

50. Mignon

Here is the story of Mignon as I remember having read it in a famous old book.

A young man named Wilhelm was staying at an inn in the city. One day as he was going upstairs he met a little girl coming down. He would have taken her for a boy, if it had not been for the long curls of black hair **wound**[①] about her head. As she ran by, he caught her in his arms and asked her to whom she belonged. He felt sure that she must be one of the rope dancers who had just come to the inn. She gave him a sharp, dark look, slipped out of his arms, and ran away without speaking.

The next time he saw her, Wilhelm spoke to her again.

"Do not be afraid of me, little one," he said kindly. "What is your name?"

"They call me Mignon," said the child.

"How old are you?" he asked.

"No one has counted," the child answered.

Wilhelm went on; but he could not help wondering about the child, and thinking of her dark eyes and strange ways.

50. 美格珑

下面这个故事的主人公叫美格珑，我记得在一本有名的旧书里读过它。

有一个名叫威尔汉姆的年轻人，住在城里的一个小旅馆里。一天，威尔汉姆上楼，正好碰到一个小女孩下楼，要不是她头上盘着长长的黑卷发，他可能会误以为她是个男孩子。就在那个小女孩从身边跑过的时候，威尔汉姆伸手抱住了她，询问她是谁家的孩子。他判断这个女孩肯定是一位走钢丝的演员，跟同伴一起刚刚在旅馆里面住下。小女孩用充满警惕和敌意的眼神望了威尔汉姆一眼，然后从他的手臂里面挣脱了出来，连一句话也没有说就跑开了。

威尔汉姆再次见到小女孩的时候，又开口跟她讲话。

"别害怕，小不点。"威尔汉姆和蔼地说，"你叫什么名字？"

"他们叫我美格珑。"那个孩子回答道。

"你几岁了？"威尔汉姆又问。

"没有人算过我的年龄。"孩子回答说。

威尔汉姆离开后，仍然无法抑制对这个孩子的好奇心，心里还在回想她的黑眼睛和那些奇怪的举动。

① wound [waund] v.（wind 的过去分词）盘绕

One day not long after that, there was a great outcry among the crowd that was watching the rope dancers. Wilhelm went down to find out what was the matter. He saw that the master of the dancers was beating little Mignon with a stick. He ran and held the man by the **collar**①.

"Let the child alone!" he cried. "If you touch her again, one of us shall never leave this spot."

The man tried to get loose; but Wilhelm held him fast. The child **crept**② away, and hid herself in the crowd.

"Pay me what her clothes cost," cried the rope dancer at last, "and you may take her."

As soon as all was quiet, Wilhelm went to look for Mignon; for she now belonged to him. But he could not find her, and it was not until the rope dancers had left the town that she came to him.

"Where have you been?" asked Wilhelm in his kindest tones; but the child did not speak.

"You are to live with me now, and you must be a good child," he said.

"I will try," said Mignon gently.

From that time she tried to do all that she could for Wilhelm and his friends. She would let no one wait on him but herself. She was often seen going to a basin of water to wash from her face the paint with which the rope dancers had reddened her cheeks: indeed, she nearly rubbed off the skin in trying to wash away its fine brown tint, which she thought was some deep dye.

Mignon grew more lovely every day. She never walked up and down the stairs, but jumped. She would spring along by the railing, and before you knew it, would be sitting quietly above on the landing.

To each one she would speak in a different way. To Wilhelm it was with her arms crossed upon her breast. Often for a whole day she would not say one word, and yet in **waiting upon**③ Wilhelm she never tired.

① collar ['kɔlə] n. 衣领

② crept [krept] v.（creep 的过去式）匍匐爬行

③ wait upon 侍候，服侍

不久后的一天，观众们正在观看走钢丝表演，突然他们中间传来一阵叫喊，威尔汉姆赶忙跑下去看究竟发生了什么事。原来，戏班的老板正在用棍子抽打小美格珑，威尔汉姆立刻冲过去抓住那个人的领子。

"放开这个孩子！"威尔汉姆叫道，"如果你再碰她一下，我们两个就会有一个人倒在这里。"

那个人竭力想挣脱出去，可是威尔汉姆的手抓得很紧。趁着这个时候，那个孩子悄悄溜出去，躲到了人群中。

"把给她买衣服的钱赔给我，"那个人大声说，"你就可以把她领走。"

等一切平静下来后，威尔汉姆去找美格珑，现在小女孩属于他了。可是不管威尔汉姆怎么找，就是找不着她。一直等到戏班出了城，美格珑才出来见他。

"这段时候你去哪儿了？"威尔汉姆用和蔼的口气问，可是那个孩子依然不说话。

"现在我们要一起生活了，你一定要做一个好孩子！"威尔汉姆说。

"我尽力吧！"美格珑轻声回应说。

从那以后，美格珑开始尽其所能为威尔汉姆和他的朋友服务，而且还不允许旁人照顾他。人们经常看见小女孩打一盆水清洗演出的时候涂在脸上的红色油彩。美格珑觉得这些油彩是一些深色的染料，为了洗去它们，几乎要把脸上的皮搓掉。

美格珑变得一天天可爱了起来，上下楼梯一步要跨好几个台阶，往往还没等随行的人反应过来，她就已经轻快地到达楼梯口的平台上了。

美格珑对不同的人有不同的说话方式。面对威尔汉姆的时候，她会把手臂抱起来放在胸前。她常常一整天不说一句话，可是照顾威尔汉姆的时候，却从来不知疲倦。

One night he came home very **weary**① and sad. Mignon was waiting for him. She carried the light before him upstairs. She set the light down upon the table, and in a little while she asked him if she might dance.

"It might ease your heart a little," she said.

Wilhelm, to please her, told her that she might.

Then she brought a little carpet, and spread it upon the floor. At each corner she placed a candle, and on the carpet she put a number of eggs. She arranged the eggs in the form of certain figures. When this was done, she called to a man who was waiting with a violin. She tied a band about her eyes, and then the dancing began.

"And then the dancing began."

How lightly, quickly, **nimbly**②, wonderfully, she moved! She skipped so fast among the eggs, she trod so closely beside them, that you would have thought she must crush them all. But not one of them did she touch. With all kinds of steps she passed among them. Not one of them was moved from its place.

Wilhelm forgot all his cares. He watched every motion of the child. He

① weary ['wiəri] *a.* 疲倦的

一天晚上威尔汉姆回到家里，身心异常疲惫。美格珑正在家里等他，提着灯笼迎他上楼。美格珑把灯放下后，问威尔汉姆能不能为他跳一支舞。

"兴许这样可以让你轻松一些。"美格珑说。

为了让美格珑高兴，威尔汉姆说当然可以。

于是美格珑取出一块地毯铺在地板上，四个角上都摆上点燃的蜡烛。然后她拿了一些鸡蛋在上面摆出一个形状，又叫来已经等在一旁的小提琴师，用布把自己的眼睛蒙上。一切准备妥当之后，美格珑便开始了舞蹈。

"美格珑便开始了舞蹈。"

② nimbly ['nimbli] *ad.* 敏捷地

美格珑的舞姿是那么轻盈敏捷、活泼美妙！她的双脚在鸡蛋中间快速移动，让人感觉她随时会把鸡蛋全部踩碎，可是她一个也没有碰到。不管跳哪种舞步，美格珑都能够避开鸡蛋，而且也没有移动任何一颗鸡蛋的位置。

威尔汉姆忘记了所有的烦恼，专注地看着孩子的每

Fifty Famous Stories Retold

almost forgot who and where he was.

When the dance was ended, Mignon rolled the eggs together with her foot into a little heap. Not one was left behind, not one was harmed. Then she took the band from her eyes, and made a little bow.

Wilhelm thanked her for showing him a dance that was so wonderful and pretty. He praised her, petted her, and hoped that she had not tired herself too much.

When she had gone from the room, the man with the violin told Wilhelm of the care she had taken to teach him the music of the dance. He told how she had sung it to him over and over again. He told how she had even wished to pay him with her own money for learning to play it for her.

There was yet another way in which Mignon tried to please Wilhelm, and make him forget his cares. She sang to him.

The song which he liked best was one whose words he had never heard before. Its music, too, was strange to him, and yet it pleased him very much. He asked her to speak the words over and over again. He wrote them down; but the sweetness of the tune was more delightful than the words. The song began in this way: —

> "Do you know the land where **citrons**[①], lemons, grow,
> And oranges under the green leaves glow?"

Once, when she had ended the song, she said again, "Do you know the land?"
"It must be Italy," said Wilhelm. "Have you ever been there?"
The child did not answer.

一个动作。他几乎忘了自己是谁，现在又身在何处。

舞蹈结束后，美格珑用脚把鸡蛋拢到一起，那些鸡蛋一颗也没有碰碎。然后她取下蒙在眼睛上的布条，向威尔汉姆微微鞠了一躬。

威尔汉姆感谢美格珑为他跳了一支如此美妙优美的舞蹈。他赞扬她、爱抚她，希望她没有累着。

一直等美格珑离开了房间，那个小提琴师才给威尔汉姆说起她教他演奏这首舞曲的事情。他说美格珑一遍又一遍地唱给他听，甚至还说要自己出钱让他学习演奏这首曲子。

歌声是美格珑让威尔汉姆开心的另一个法宝。

有一首歌是威尔汉姆最喜欢的。威尔汉姆以前从来没有听到过这首歌的歌词，乐曲对他来说也很陌生，可是他却非常喜爱它，让美格珑一遍又一遍把歌词重复给他听，并且还把歌词写了下来。那首歌不仅歌词优美，曲调也更加动人。歌的开头是这样的：

"你可知道那个生长着香橼和柠檬的地方？
那里还有橘子在绿叶中发亮。"

① citron ['sitrən] *n.* 香橼

有一次，美格珑唱完这首歌之后又像以往一样问他："你知道这个地方吗？"

"这个地方一定是意大利。"威尔汉姆说，"你去过那里没有？"

可是孩子并没有回答。